CW00545940
WANTED
FEIJOAS
REWARD

Dear Lorraine

Happy (super belated) 40th birthday!

This is my favourite kiwi cookbook from my favourite kiwi deli. May it provide some inspiration for Paul Mary's and the Hummingbird Deli.

Love

Carolyn xx

xx

Ripe
RECIPES

Angela Redfern

Illustrations by Michelle Ineson

PHOTOGRAPHY BY SALLY GREER

Beatnik
Publishing

This book is dedicated to Rose, her owl, fruit cake recipes and my little sister.

First published in 2010 by Beatnik Publishing in association with Ripe Delicatessen.
Revised and reprinted in 2011 by Beatnik Publishing in association with Ripe Delicatessen.
Revised and reprinted in 2013 by Beatnik Publishing in association with Ripe Delicatessen.
Reprinted in 2014 by Beatnik Publishing in association with Ripe Delicatessen.

Managing Editor & Researcher: Karla Granville

Designers: Sally Greer & Colette Sherley

Recipe Development, Food Styling & Testing: Ripe Delicatessen

Chefs: Andrea Saunders, Lynn Colbert, Amy Melchior, Pip Wylie, Kylie Wilson,
Gemma Heffernan, John Utumapu, John-Henry Rand, Tina Brown, Louise Kelleher, Karla Granville
Recipe Testing: Bik Yimdee, Sally Cameron, Jo Bridgeford, Stacy Devoy

Printed and bound in China.

ISBN 978-0-473-17347-0

PO Box 8276, Symonds Street
Auckland 1150, New Zealand

www.beatnikpublishing.com

Ripe Delicatessen
172 Richmond Rd, Grey Lynn, Auckland

www.ripedeli.co.nz

CONTENTS

Every season has its charms.

Small

Medium

* LARGE $14.00

INTRODUCTION

THE BEGINNING

I would like to be able to say I had an epiphany and woke up one morning aged 10 thinking "I'm going to be a cook", but I'm afraid nothing as clichéd as that happened.

I do, however, remember tucking into mum's dinners with delight and I have many fond memories of licking the bowl after a burst of her baking.

Basically, my culinary skills were passed down by my mother who spent numerous hours in the kitchen. Added to the fact that I was never going to make it academically (surely you can't be academic and creative!), cooking school seemed like the natural choice for me.

A hospitality management course set the ground work before I was singled out and offered a work placement at the Savoy Hotel in London. That was when I really got excited about food and cooking and where the foundations of understanding the ins and outs of a kitchen began. The standards, the discipline, the adrenalin, the crazy French chef (I couldn't understand a word!), all cemented my desire to continue in the culinary world.

It was working at Designers Guild under the guidance of Tricia Guild that really opened my eyes to all the other aspects of running a café. From the way the food was presented, to the design of the store, to creating the right atmosphere – her passion and attention to detail were truly inspiring.

But it was in New Zealand where I finally figured out what I really wanted to do. Having worked in the likes of Pasta Italia and Zarbo I realised that "going deli" was the life for me. So, on a whim and a prayer, a shoestring budget, plenty of help from friends and family – and the fact that I just wanted to make great food! – Ripe was born.

It was September 2002 when I first opened the doors to Ripe on the site of an old burger joint – Georges Burgers on Richmond Road. I didn't know exactly what was ahead of me but I did know I wanted to offer home-made style, quality, take-out food. I just knew it was right, and I hoped my customers thought so too. Luckily for me they did, and before I knew it I had secured the old Indian takeaway site just down the road where the larger, grander Ripe now stands.

And now a book – *Ripe Recipes*. Why? Because we thought it would be a lot of fun, because our wonderful customers often ask us for our recipes and because my co-workers are so fantastic and creative that we thought we would bring a little bit of Ripe goodness into your own home.

GETTING IT RIPE – SEASONAL COOKING

Ripe's philosophy is simple: fresh, quality, seasonal, healthy food that's good value for money. It's all about getting back to basics, creating simple, tasty fare and thinking about where your food comes from.

We live in the world of *now*, where everything is at our fingertips and every option is afforded to us. The supermarket is adorned with every fruit and vegetable of every kind from every country. We say "Slow down. Smell the locally grown apples."

Knowing how to cook seasonally means you'll be able to turn all sorts of fresh ingredients into meals when they're at their best, and cheapest. And that's why we decided to base this book on seasonal cooking.

To be honest, this has been a big learning curve for us. You would think people in our industry would know all about what's in season, but with everything available on our shelves all year round it can be hard to decipher one season from the next!

What we do know is that the choices we make as we shop are the overriding factors that will affect the way our food tastes. Therefore, seasonality just makes sense. It means that we're tasting nature's finest when it's at its best, as well as supporting local producers.

HOW TO USE THIS BOOK

This book is not about fuss and bother. It's not about making everything from scratch. In fact, you will find in some of the recipes we have included ready-made pastry and stock.

On the other hand, some recipes are more in-depth and you may have to spend a little more time to get that something really special (like our rhubarb butterscotch cake). Just get a friend round, pour another glass of wine and enjoy the process!

You will see from the design of the book that it is broken up into seasonal sections. This is intended as a guideline only, as many products can extend into other months. However, if you do follow the book you will be cooking most things in season, meaning they will taste their best and be at their cheapest and you'll also have a nice well-stocked cupboard of preserves at the end of the year. Who wouldn't be proud of that!

A FEW TIPS

- Please read the recipe through completely before you start. We found this helps to get a good understanding before you begin the cooking process and eliminates any surprises.
- It is also a very good idea to have everything ready before you begin, for example, onions chopped, tins opened, flour weighed, oven preheated. An organised approach makes cooking and baking run a lot smoother.
- Please read through our tips at the back for help and guidance.
- Butter and salt are your friends, like anything in moderation. Salt is especially essential for bringing out the flavour of your food.
- We love fresh herbs – use lots, it makes all the difference.
- Don't be afraid to try the recipes even if they look complicated. Cooking should be about relaxing and having fun so when you find yourself beating the mashed potato to the point of cardiac arrest – stop!
- Remember that individual ovens vary. The cooking times stated are from our ovens so you need to get to know the quirks of your own.
- Some of the recipe photographs are of large deli sized quantities and do not reflect the amount of food the recipe will actually produce.
- There is Ripe specific conversion charts located on page 212
- Cup measurements are not tightly packed.
- Share the love and use free-farmed foods. We do.
- Remember, "To eat is a necessity, but to eat intelligently is an art."

"As I get older I notice the years less and the seasons more." – John Hubbard

ANTIPASTO

Always appreciated.

"Let's get this show on the road." – Ginny Kevey

ANTIPASTO

It's always a good idea to have a few things in the fridge that keep well for last minute antipasto platters – making finger food from scratch when your guests are already arriving isn't always fun.

So we have given a few recipes here for pestos, tapenade, pâté and dips you can make at your convenience and keep on hand.

Our simple finger food items look great on a platter, either on their own, or offered with the produce suggestions below. Visually, we find it more appealing to limit your number of choices and increase the quantities of each.

Occasionally we use foliage from the garden such as banana, flax and grape vine leaves to line the platter, and of course lots of fresh herbs to garnish.

Keep it simple. A couple of yummy cheeses, a fruit paste and some good crackers or Parmesan biscuits are a good base to your platter.

Here are a few more ideas for foods you can add:

> Cured meats, semi dried tomatoes, caper berries, olives, cornichons, marinated artichokes, sardines, anchovies, smoked fish, smoked mussels, pickles, chutneys, pestos, roasted peppers, courgettes and bruschetta.

As most of these food items store well, it would be a good idea to keep a small selection in your pantry.

Crudités, which are chopped up fresh raw vegetables, make a great accompaniment to serve with dips. Not only are they good for you but they add colour and texture to your platter too. Mix these with fresh bread or crackers.

Try these crudité suggestions:

> Cherry tomatoes, celery, broccoli, carrots, fennel, courgettes, cauliflower, snow peas, capsicums.

Use your creative flair with arranging the food – you can't go wrong!

PEA, MINT & FETA FRITTERS

Fantastic as finger food, or make larger ones for more substantial servings.

Makes 25-30 small fritters.

PEA FRITTERS

400g **PEAS**, *fresh or frozen*
5 **EGGS**, *separated*
2 **SPRING ONIONS**, *very thinly sliced*
2 tbsp **FRESH MINT LEAVES**, *roughly chopped*
100g **FETA**, *crumbled*
ZEST *of 3* **LEMONS**
½ tsp **GROUND CUMIN**
1 cup (80g) **FRESH BREAD CRUMBS**
2 tsp **BAKING POWDER**
OLIVE OIL, *for shallow frying*
1 cup **FRESH MINT LEAVES**, *to serve*

CITRUS DIPPING SAUCE

250g **CRÈME FRAICHE**
2 tbsp **PLAIN UNSWEETENED YOGHURT**
JUICE *of 1* **LEMON**
1 clove **GARLIC**, *crushed*
1 tbsp **FRESH MINT LEAVES**, *finely chopped*
SALT *and freshly* **GROUND BLACK PEPPER**

To prepare the fritters: bring a large saucepan of water to the boil and cook the peas for 3-4 minutes or until tender.

Drain and mash coarsely using a fork or potato masher.

In a large bowl, whisk egg yolks until frothy.

Add to the egg yolks the mashed peas, spring onions, mint, crumbled feta, lemon zest, cumin, bread crumbs, baking powder and salt and pepper to season. Stir to combine.

In a clean, dry bowl, whisk the egg whites until soft peaks form. Fold the whites gently into the pea mixture in three batches until just combined.

In a large frying pan, heat ½ cm of oil to a medium heat and shallow fry heaped tablespoons of the mixture for 1 minute each side or until golden brown.

Line an oven tray with baking paper and keep the fritters warm in a low oven (150°C) while frying the remaining mixture.

Serve with the citrus dipping sauce and plenty of fresh mint leaves.

To prepare the citrus dipping sauce: place all the ingredients into a bowl. Mix well to combine.

Season to taste with salt and pepper and keep in the fridge until needed.

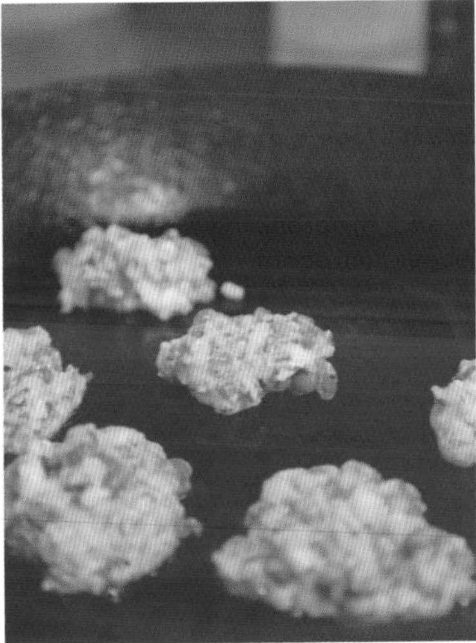

STUFFED MUSHROOMS

8 large ***FIELD MUSHROOMS****, brushed clean*
½ small ***RED ONION****, peeled, finely chopped*
¼ cup (20g) ***PINENUTS****, roughly chopped*
120g ***FETA****, crumbled*
½ tsp freshly ***GROUND BLACK PEPPER***
1 small handful of ***BABY SPINACH LEAVES****, roughly chopped*
¼ cup (20g) ***PARMESAN****, grated*
¼ cup (60ml) ***OLIVE OIL***

Preheat oven to 180°C.

Remove the mushroom stalks and arrange on an oven tray lined with baking paper, stalk sides facing up. In a bowl mix together the red onion, pinenuts, feta, pepper and baby spinach.

Divide the mixture into eight and mound a portion of the stuffing on top of each mushroom, pressing down lightly to secure the filling.

Sprinkle with Parmesan.

Drizzle olive oil all over and bake for 20 minutes.

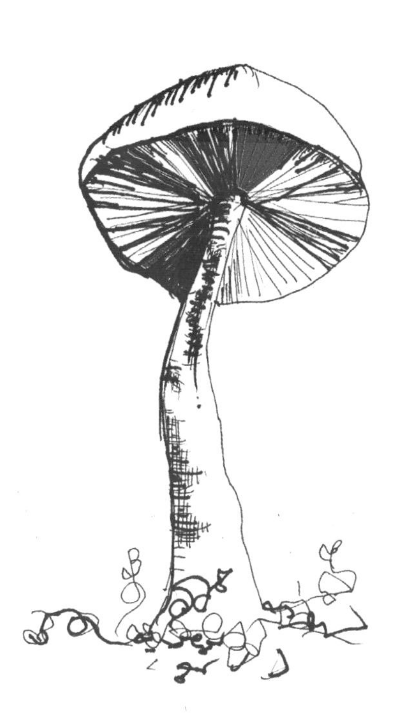

FILLED PEPPADEWS

250g ***CREAM CHEESE****, softened*
100g cow or goat ***FETA****, crumbled*
½ cup ***FRESH HERBS****, such as basil, parsley, coriander or chives, finely chopped*
1 tsp freshly ***GROUND BLACK PEPPER***
SALT *if needed*
400g (approx 30) jar of ***PEPPADEWS***
OLIVE OIL*, for drizzling*

Beat the cream cheese and feta with a wooden spoon until smooth.

Add the finely chopped fresh herbs and the freshly ground black pepper. Mix to combine, taste and add salt if needed.

Transfer the mixture to a piping bag and fill the peppadews. Place in a shallow dish and drizzle olive oil over and serve as part of an antipasto selection or alone as a tasty snack.

Filled peppadews will store for up to 2 weeks in the fridge, covered with oil in a sealed container.

ASIAN BUTTON MUSHROOMS

Serves 4-6

500g (approx 30) ***BUTTON MUSHROOMS****, brushed clean*
3 tbsp ***SESAME OIL***
¼ cup (60ml) ***SWEET SOY SAUCE***
¼ cup (60ml) ***SWEET CHILLI SAUCE***
1 tbsp ***FRESH GINGER****, grated*
¼ cup (30g) ***SESAME SEEDS***
1 cup of ***FRESH CORIANDER LEAVES****, roughly chopped*

Preheat oven to 180°C.

Place cleaned mushrooms into a deep sided oven dish.

Combine the sesame oil, soy sauce, sweet chilli, and grated ginger in a small jug or bowl.

Pour over the mushrooms and toss to cover evenly with sauce.

Sprinkle over the sesame seeds and half of the chopped coriander.

Roast in the oven until the mushrooms have browned, approximately 40 minutes.

Once the mushrooms have cooled a little, sprinkle the other half of the chopped coriander over the top. Delicious served as an antipasto or toss through salads.

CHEESY SHORTBREAD

Thank you Sallyann Hingston for this recipe. And for the many enjoyable hours I spent working alongside you at Ripe.

Makes around 20

120g ***BLUE CHEESE***
1½ cup (120g) ***PARMESAN CHEESE****, grated*
120g ***UNSALTED BUTTER****, softened*
1 large ***EGG***
125g plain ***FLOUR***
Freshly ***GROUND BLACK PEPPER***
2 tbsp ***CARAWAY*** *or black sesame seeds*

In a food processor bowl, put together the cheeses and butter and blend until smooth. Add the egg and blend.

Remove from food processor bowl and transfer to a mixing bowl. Fold in the flour and pepper. Divide the mixture in half and shape into two logs.

Sprinkle the toasted seeds onto a baking paper sheet and roll the logs in the seeds to coat. Wrap seeded logs in cling film and put in the freezer to chill for 15 minutes. If you like, you can freeze one of the logs completely and use it at a later date.

Preheat oven to 180°C while logs are chilling.

Line two baking trays with baking paper.

Take the logs from the freezer, remove the cling wrap and cut into slices no more than 5mm thick.

Place cut slices onto the lined baking trays and bake until golden, approximately 15 minutes.

Cool on the baking trays for extra crispness and store in air tight containers.

BASIL PESTO

4 cups ***FRESH BASIL LEAVES***
1 cup (80g) ***PARMESAN CHEESE****, grated*
4 cloves ***GARLIC****, peeled*
½ cup (75g) ***NUTS*** *or seeds, e.g. almonds, pinenuts, sunflower seeds or pumpkin seeds*
1½ cups (375ml) a mix of ***OLIVE OIL*** *and a light* ***VEGETABLE OIL***
½ tsp ***SALT****, or to taste*

Toast the nuts or seeds (see pg 211).

In a food processor bowl, place the basil leaves, Parmesan, garlic and nuts or seeds.

Whilst the food processor is running, slowly pour in the oil until a thick paste is formed. Season with salt.

Store covered in the fridge.

SUNDRIED TOMATO PESTO

3 sprigs ***FRESH ROSEMARY****, leaves picked and finely chopped*
½ cup (75g) raw ***ALMONDS***
2 cups (320g) ***SUNDRIED TOMATOES****, drained of oil*
½ cup (125ml) a mix of ***OLIVE OIL*** *and a light* ***VEGETABLE OIL***
1 cup ***FRESH PARSLEY****, roughly chopped*
½ cup (40g) ***PARMESAN****, grated*

Preheat oven to 200°C.

Toast the rosemary and almonds on an oven tray for about 5 minutes.

Place all ingredients into a food processor bowl. Blend until combined and the mixture is the consistency of a rough paste.

Store covered in the fridge.

OLIVE TAPENADE

2 tbsp ***OLIVE OIL***
1 bulb of ***GARLIC****, broken into cloves, skin on*
2 cups (330g) ***KALAMATA OLIVES****, stones removed*
6 ***ANCHOVY FILLETS***

Preheat oven to 180°C.

Toss all the ingredients in the oil and roast on a tray for 10-15 minutes or until the garlic is soft then remove from the oven. Once the garlic has cooled squeeze it to remove the skin.

Place the roasted olive mixture and garlic into the bowl of a food processor. Purée until smooth and thick.

Store covered in the fridge.

Pesto is something everyone loves stirred through fresh pasta. Make bruschetta by spreading pesto on pieces of bread, sprinkling with Parmesan, then baking in a medium oven until crisp – a great way to use leftover bread.

ASPARAGUS PROSCIUTTO

*15 **ASPARAGUS SPEARS**, trim woody ends*
*½ cup **OLIVE TAPENADE**, or sun dried tomato pesto (see pg 16)*
*15 **PROSCIUTTO** slices*
*Dash of **VEGETABLE OIL***

Place a large pot of water over high heat, bring to the boil and blanch the asparagus spears for 1 minute. Refresh in iced cold water, drain and set aside.

Spread 1 tsp of tapenade down the length of one side of each prosciutto strip. Fold the other side over so the tapenade is trapped. Roll the prosciutto around the length of the asparagus, starting from the bottom and leaving the tip exposed.

Heat a frying pan with the dash of olive oil over medium heat. Fry asparagus until the prosciutto is crispy at the edges. This takes approximately 30 seconds.

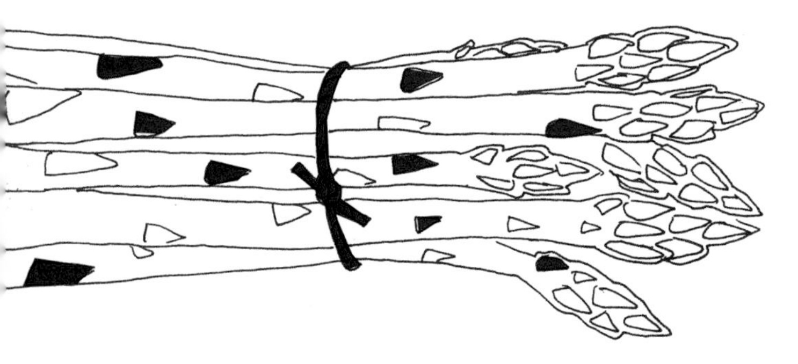

CHICKEN LIVER PÂTÉ

This recipe also benefits from the addition of roasted cashews or shelled hazelnuts – mix a ½ cup of nuts into pâté when blending.

Seasoning is essential – salt really brings out the flavour along with lots of freshly ground black pepper. A great gift when served in pretty ramekins.

*350g fresh **CHICKEN LIVERS***
*100g **BUTTER***
*1 **ONION**, peeled, finely sliced*
*4 cloves **GARLIC**, finely diced*
*¼ cup **FRESH THYME LEAVES**, chopped*
*⅓ cup (80ml) **PORT** or brandy*
*½ cup (125ml) **CREAM***
*½ tsp **SALT***
*½ tsp freshly **GROUND BLACK PEPPER***
*50g second measure of **BUTTER**, for preserving*
*1 tbsp **PINK** and **GREEN PEPPERCORNS***

Clean the livers and remove any sinew or fat then roughly chop.

In a large frying pan, over a medium to high heat melt the first measure of butter. When bubbling, add livers, onion, garlic and thyme.

Cook for 5-7 minutes or until the livers have turned a pale pink colour and the mixture has started to caramelise. At this point, add the port and cook for a minute on a high heat to burn off the alcohol.

Stir in the cream and seasonings. Simmer for 3-5 minutes while liquid reduces and thickens.

Pour pâté mixture into a food processor bowl and blend until smooth. Taste and check for seasoning.

Pour into a serving dish and smooth the top with a spatula. Melt the second measure of butter and pour over the pâté.

Sprinkle the peppercorns over the top. Leave to set and keep chilled in the fridge.

BEET CURED SALMON

Slice thinly and serve with anything your heart desires. Great as part of antipasto platters, with scrambled eggs, or as part of a salad with lots of fresh rocket and herbs.

500g piece ***SALMON TAIL*** *(a good piece with minimal bones), skin on*
1 raw ***BEETROOT****, grated*
2 tbsp (30g) ***SEA SALT FLAKES***
2 tbsp (30g) ***WHITE SUGAR***
ZEST *of ½* ***LIME***
2 tbsp ***FRESH FENNEL LEAVES*** *or dill, finely chopped*
1 tsp ***VANILLA EXTRACT***
1 tbsp ***VODKA***

Feel the salmon for bones with fingertips; if any are found remove with tweezers.

In a bowl mix together the grated beetroot with salt, sugar, lime zest, fennel or dill, vanilla and vodka.

Lie the salmon skin side down on a large piece of cling wrap and place in a container just slightly bigger than the salmon piece. A pretty snug fit is what you are after.

Press the curing mixture onto the top of the salmon, making sure it's totally covered. Wrap the excess cling wrap tightly over the salmon to seal. Place a flat heavy object over the salmon to weigh it down.

Cure for 24-48 hours. The longer you are able to leave the curing mixture on the salmon, the deeper the beetroot colour will be, resulting in a fantastic ruby shade.

When ready to use, unwrap the salmon and remove the curing mixture with cold water, patting dry with paper towels.

Slice very thinly as it is very rich.

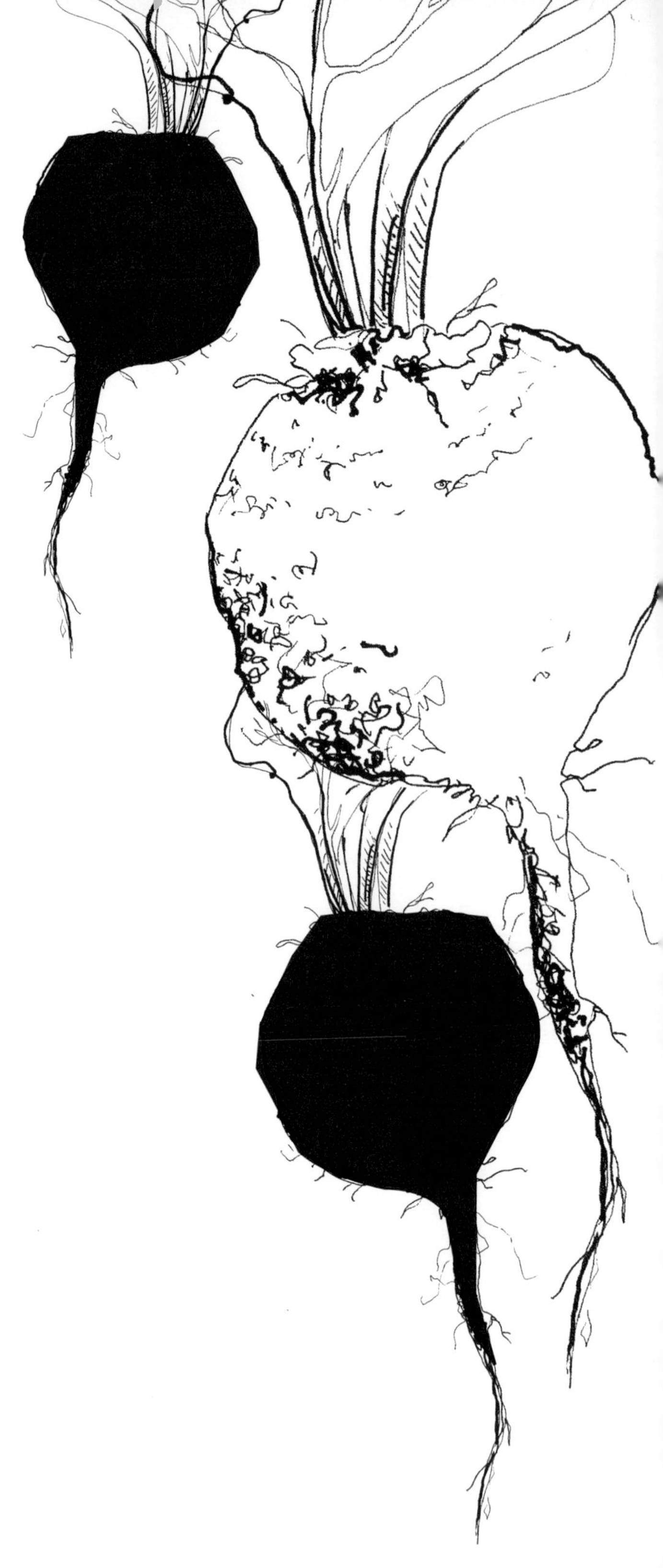

"This knife is so blunt it wouldn't cut butter." – Theo Paddy

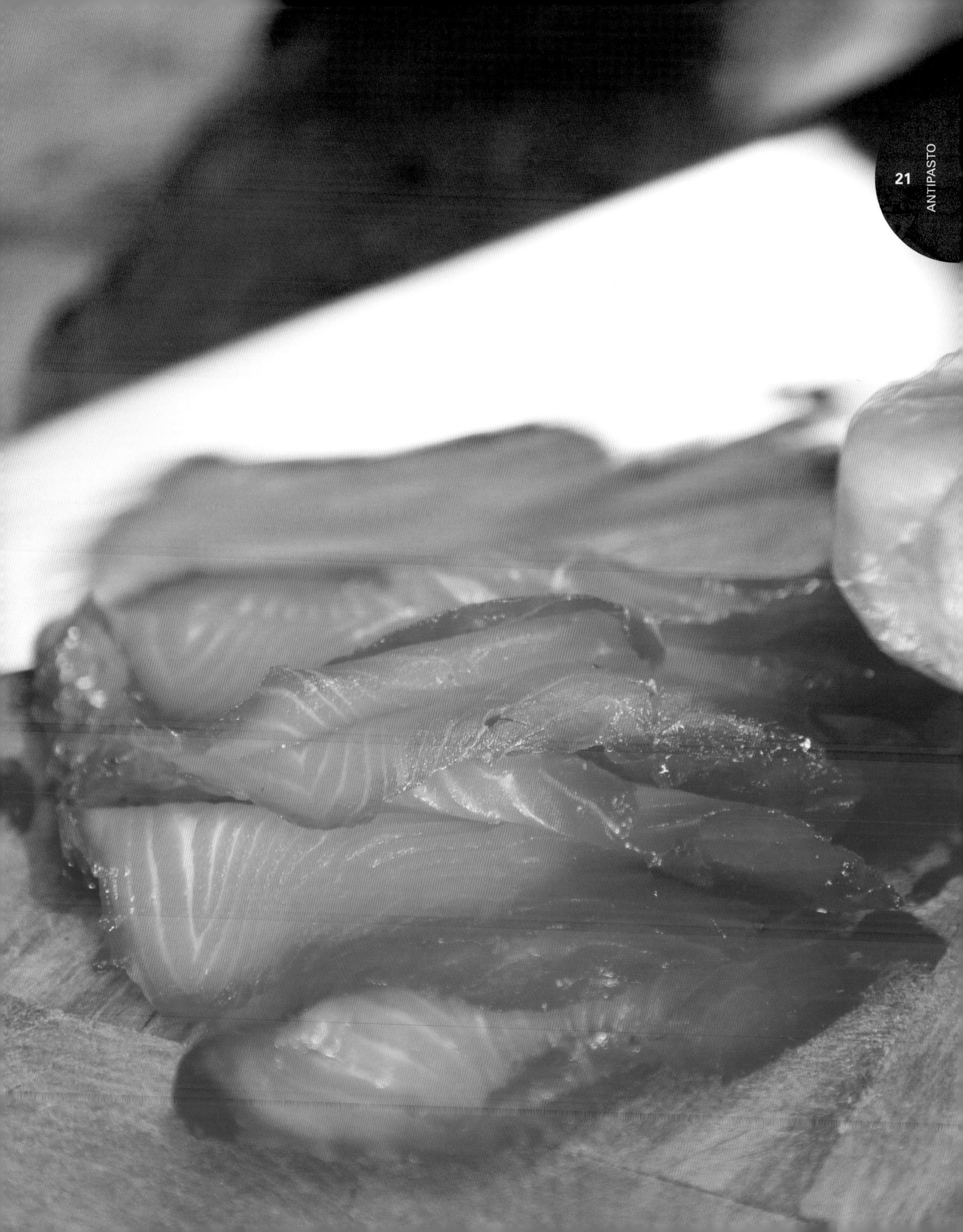

CORIANDER, SWEET CHILLI & PEANUT DIP

1 cup ***FRESH CORIANDER LEAVES***
1 cup ***FRESH MINT LEAVES***
JUICE *and* ***ZEST*** *of 1* ***LEMON***
3 tbsp ***SWEET CHILLI SAUCE***
2 tsp ***FISH SAUCE***
½ cup (75g) ***UNSALTED PEANUTS****, toasted*
2 tbsp ***SESAME OIL***
SALT *and freshly* ***GROUND BLACK PEPPER***

In a bowl, place the fresh herbs, lemon zest, sweet chilli sauce, fish sauce, peanuts and sesame oil.

Using a stick blender, blitz to a rough paste. Season with salt and pepper and add lemon juice to taste.

Store covered in the fridge.

BLUE CHEESE, BRANDY & CASHEW DIP

130g of your favourite ***BLUE CHEESE***
250g ***CREAM CHEESE***
⅓ cup (80ml) ***CREAM***
2 tbsp ***BRANDY***
50g ***CASHEW NUTS****, toasted (see pg 211), roughly chopped*
SALT *and freshly* ***GROUND BLACK PEPPER***

In a food processor bowl, combine all the ingredients and blend until smooth. Season with salt and pepper to taste.

Store covered in the fridge.

GOATS' FETA & MINT DIP

200g ***GOATS' FETA*** *cheese*
250g ***SOUR CREAM***
JUICE *and* ***ZEST*** *of 2* ***LEMONS***
¼ cup ***FRESH MINT LEAVES****, roughly chopped*
½ tsp freshly ***GROUND BLACK PEPPER***

In a food processor bowl place the feta, sour cream, lemon juice and zest. Blend until smooth, empty the mixture into a bowl and stir in fresh mint leaves and pepper.

Store covered in the fridge.

RED CAPSICUM & BASIL DIP

4 large ***RED CAPSICUMS****, cut in half, membranes removed*
1 tbsp ***VEGETABLE OIL***
3 cloves ***GARLIC****, peeled*
1 cup ***FRESH BASIL LEAVES***
1 tsp ***HONEY***
Squeeze of ***LEMON JUICE***
⅓ cup (80ml) ***OLIVE OIL***
SALT *and freshly* ***GROUND BLACK PEPPER***
Extra vegetable oil for preserving

Preheat oven to 180°C.

Line an oven tray with baking paper and arrange capsicum halves skin side up. Drizzle with vegetable oil and rub onto the skin. Roast until the skins have darkened – this takes approximately 30 minutes.

Remove tray from oven and place hot capsicums in a large bowl. Cover with cling film and allow to cool. Once cooled, peel the skins off.

In a food processor bowl, place the peeled capsicums, garlic, basil, honey and lemon juice and blend to a smooth consistency. Slowly add the olive oil to emulsify.

Season with salt and pepper to taste.

To store, pour into a jar and cover with vegetable oil. This prevents the basil browning. Keep refrigerated.

Peas.Apricots.
Beans.Cucumbers.
Corn.Capsicum.
Peaches.Chillies.
Blueberries.Florence
fennel.Pomegranate.
Cherries.Eggplant.
Lettuce.Rocket.Snow
peas.Strawberries.
Currants.Tomatoes.
Radish.Spinach.
Raspberries.
Blackberries.

DECEMBER | JANUARY

Try out salads with fresh summer vegetables and mix them up with grains and seeds.

INSALATA CAPRESE

We wanted to include this recipe to make the most of ripe tomatoes at this time of the year. We recommend tasty buffalo mozzarella which is now made here in New Zealand.

This recipe is so gloriously simple, but it does require perfect ingredients. Arrange on the plate however you like and serve with crusty bread.

8 medium vine ripened ***TOMATOES***
300g fresh ***BUFFALO MOZZARELLA***
1 large handful of ***FRESH BASIL LEAVES***
½ cup (125ml) ***BASIL DRESSING*** *(see pg 203) or a drizzle of good extra virgin olive oil and a splash of balsamic vinegar*
SALT *and freshly* ***GROUND BLACK PEPPER***

Slice the tomatoes and tear the mozzarella and the basil leaves into bite sized pieces.

Arrange the ingredients onto a platter and drizzle with basil dressing or olive oil. Season with salt and pepper.

"Tell me what you eat, and I will tell you what you are." – Anthelme Brillat-Savarin

CHICKEN BREASTS STUFFED WITH SILVERBEET, COTTAGE CHEESE & PINENUTS

Serves 4-6

*100g **SILVERBEET**, green part only, finely sliced*
*250g **COTTAGE CHEESE***
*¼ tsp freshly grated or dried **NUTMEG***
*100g **FETA** cheese*
*⅓ cup (30g) **PINENUTS***
ZEST** of 1 **LEMON
*¼ tsp **SALT***
*Freshly **GROUND BLACK PEPPER***
*4-6 large **CHICKEN BREASTS**, skin on*
***OLIVE OIL** for drizzling*

Preheat oven to 180°C.

In a bowl combine together the silverbeet, cottage cheese, nutmeg, feta, pinenuts, lemon zest, salt and pepper. Evenly divide the stuffing mixture and spread carefully under the skin of the chicken breasts.

Place the chicken breasts in a deep sided oven tray, skin side up. Sprinkle with salt and pepper and drizzle with oil. Bake for 45 minutes or until the juices run clear.

Drain excess liquid before serving.

QUINOA CRUSTED SALMON

Using quinoa is a great alternative to bread crumbs. Red and white quinoa both work very well.

Serves 6

*⅓ cup (70g) **QUINOA***
*1 cup **FRESH DILL**, finely chopped*
*1 cup **FRESH ITALIAN PARSLEY**, finely chopped*
JUICE** and **ZEST** of 2 **LEMONS
*¼ cup (40g) **CAPERS**, finely chopped*
*1kg **SALMON FILLET**, skin on, cut into portions*
SEA SALT FLAKES** and freshly **GROUND BLACK PEPPER

Preheat oven to 180°C.

Cook the quinoa (see pg 211).

In a bowl, combine half of the fresh herbs with the quinoa, lemon zest, juice and capers.

Lightly grease an oven tray. Place the salmon skin side down and sprinkle with salt flakes and pepper. Press the quinoa mixture onto the salmon fillets.

Bake in the oven for 15 minutes or until the salmon is cooked to your liking.

Remove from oven and sprinkle with the remaining herbs to serve.

SMOKED FISH & ASPARAGUS SALAD

A delicious salad to make with your favourite smoked fish. We use a lot of smoked fish from the Coromandel Smoking Co. Its vacuum packed, a good keeper, and can be bought on-line.

Serve with a big bowl of steaming buttered new potatoes and sweet corn cobs.

Serves 4-6

*500g **ASPARAGUS SPEARS**, trim woody ends and slice in half on an angle*
*500g good quality, **SMOKED FISH** (snapper, trevally, mackerel are good)*
*½ **RED ONION**, peeled, finely sliced*
*1 cup (165g) **KALAMATA OLIVES***
*¾ cup **DILL DRESSING** (see pg 202)*
*½ cup **FRESH ITALIAN PARSLEY**, roughly chopped*
SALT** and freshly **GROUND BLACK PEPPER
*4 **EGGS**, hard boiled, shelled and quartered*
JUICE** of 1 **LEMON
*garnish with **FRESH DILL***

Bring a saucepan of water to boil and blanch the asparagus for approximately 40 seconds, remove with a slotted spoon and refresh in iced cold water. Drain and set aside.

In a large mixing bowl, shred the smoked fish, add the red onion, olives, asparagus, dressing and parsley. Season with salt and pepper and toss gently.

Place on a serving dish and arrange the eggs over the salad. Finish with a squeeze of fresh lemon juice and dill to garnish.

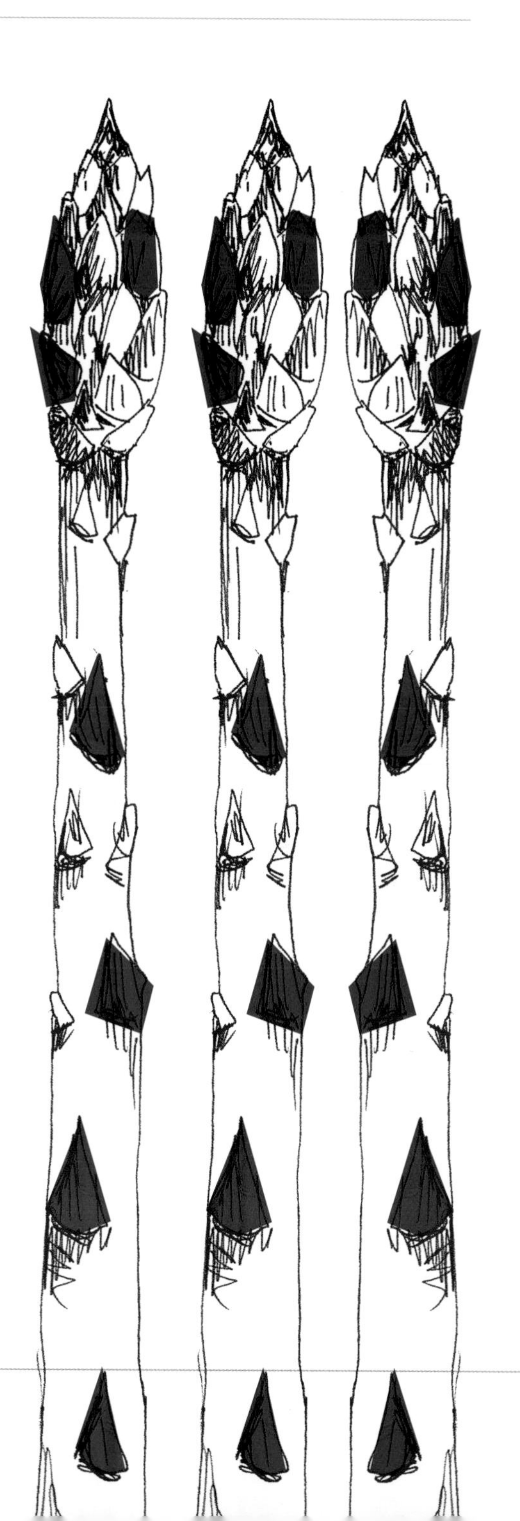

CHICKPEA CUCUMBER SALAD WITH GOATS' CHEESE DRESSING

One of our very talented chefs, John-Henry Rand (JH to those who know him) created this wonderful salad. Cows feta is a good replacement for the goats' cheese. Thank you JH.

Serves 6

CHICKPEA CUCUMBER SALAD

1 cup (200g) **CHICKPEAS**, *soaked overnight*
100g **GREEN BEANS**, *cut into 3*
2 ripe **AVOCADOS**
JUICE *of 2* **LEMONS**
½ cup **FRESH ITALIAN PARSLEY**, *roughly chopped*
½ cup **FRESH MINT LEAVES**, *roughly chopped*
½ **TELEGRAPH CUCUMBER**, *sliced into rounds*
¼ **RED ONION**, *peeled, sliced thinly*
2 stalks **CELERY**, *thinly sliced*
1 large handful of **FRESH ROCKET LEAVES** *or baby spinach*
2 tbsp **EXTRA VIRGIN OLIVE OIL**
SALT *and freshly* **GROUND BLACK PEPPER**

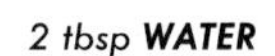

GOATS' CHEESE DRESSING

1 clove **GARLIC**, *crushed*
1 tbsp **TAHINI**
JUICE *of 1* **LEMON**
75g soft **GOATS' CHEESE** *or feta*
¼ cup (60ml) **YOGHURT**
2 tbsp **WATER**

Cook the chickpeas (see pg 210).

Blanch the beans in a saucepan of boiling water for 2-3 minutes, drain and refresh in iced cold water and drain again.

Peel and cut the avocado into bite sized pieces and toss with the lemon juice to prevent browning.

In a large bowl combine the chickpeas, green beans, sliced avocado, lemon juice, fresh herbs, cucumber, red onion, celery and rocket or spinach leaves. Toss with the olive oil and season with salt and pepper.

Arrange on a platter and drizzle generously with the goats' cheese dressing.

Store any excess dressing in the fridge for up to 5 days.

To prepare the dressing: place the garlic, tahini, lemon juice, goats cheese, yoghurt and water into a food processor bowl and blend together.

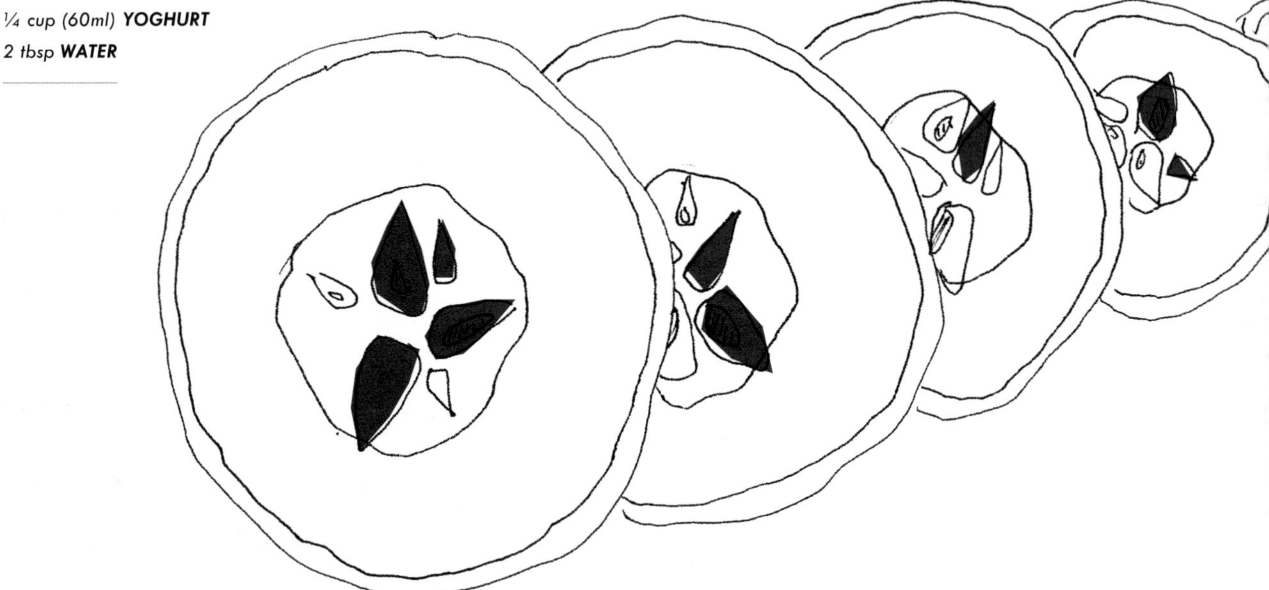

CHRISTMAS BROCCOLI SALAD

A festive coloured salad that is bursting with goodness. This is one of the many eye-catching and flavourful salad recipes that Andrea Saunders has created for this book. Her creativity with preparing salads has been inspiring to her colleagues and eagerly devoured by our customers.

Serves 4-6

3 medium sized ***RED CAPSICUMS***
OLIVE OIL
SALT *and freshly* ***GROUND BLACK PEPPER***
250g ***ASPARAGUS****, chopped in half on an angle*
1 large head of ***BROCCOLI****, cut into florets*
500g ***GREEN BEANS****, trimmed*
½ cup (60g) whole ***ALMONDS****, toasted in oven*
250g ***CREAMY FETA*** *cheese, roughly diced*
1 cup (250ml) ***BASIL DRESSING*** *(see pg 203)*

Preheat oven to 180°C.

Prepare the capsicums by removing stalks and seeds and cutting into large bite sized pieces.

Toss capsicums in a dash of olive oil, salt and pepper and place on an oven tray. Roast for 20 minutes or until tender and just starting to brown. Remove from oven and allow to cool.

To blanch vegetables: bring a large pot of water to the boil over a high heat. Place the asparagus in the boiling water for approximately 40 seconds. Then refresh in iced cold water, drain and set aside. Repeat the process with the broccoli and beans, cooking for 1-2 minutes. Blanching will leave your vegetables crunchy, so if you prefer a softer bite, boil for slightly longer.

Ensure all the vegetables are drained well. Pat dry with a clean cloth if necessary.

In a large serving bowl or platter, place all the vegetables together with the almonds, feta, and basil dressing and toss.

Season with salt and pepper to taste.

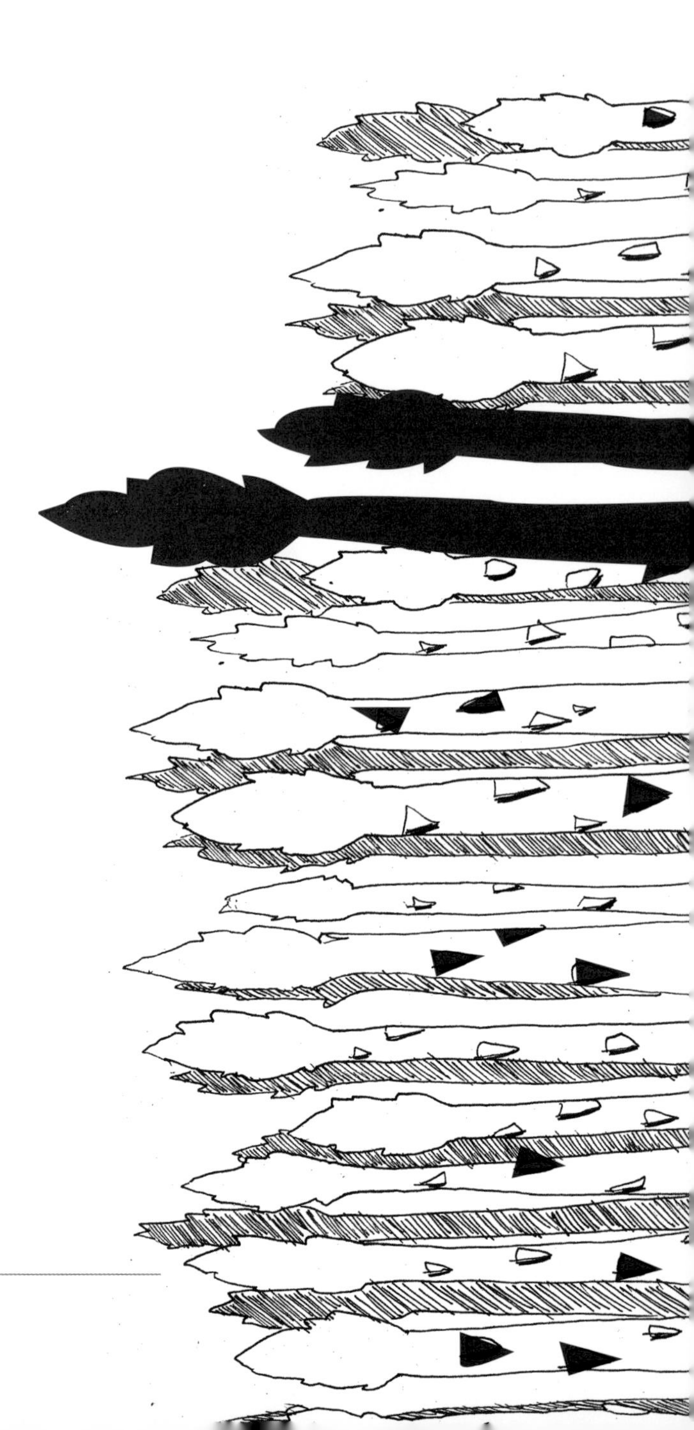

GREEN SUMMER ORZO SALAD

A great salad suitable for any type of pasta.

Serves 4-6

2 cups (400g) ***ORZO***
200g ***HALOUMI****, cut into small squares*
1 cup (80g) ***PARMESAN****, grated*
SALT *and freshly* ***GROUND BLACK PEPPER***
2 cups (500ml) ***GREEN HERB DRESSING***

GREEN HERB DRESSING

1 cup ***FRESH MINT LEAVES****, roughly chopped*
1 cup ***FRESH BASIL LEAVES****, roughly chopped*
1 cup ***FRESH ROCKET****, roughly chopped*
1 cup ***FRESH ITALIAN PARSLEY****, roughly chopped*
5 CAPER BERRIES
5 ANCHOVY FILLETS
JUICE *of 3* ***LEMONS, ZEST*** *of 2 lemons*
1 cup (250ml) ***OLIVE OIL***
¼ ***RED ONION****, finely diced*
2 tsp ***SALT***
1 ***FRESH CHILLI****, seeds removed, finely chopped*
2 tbsp ***WHITE WINE VINEGAR***

Cook the orzo (see pg 211).

In a small frying pan over high heat, fry the haloumi until melting and beginning to turn golden, turning once.

In a large serving bowl stir the green herb dressing through the cooked orzo. Taste and season with salt and pepper as desired. Scatter with the cooked haloumi and sprinkle on the Parmesan.

To prepare the dressing: using a food processor or a stick blender, combine all the green herb dressing ingredients and process until thick.

SMOKY MOROCCAN QUINOA SALAD

Serves 4-6

⅓ cup (70g) ***CHICKPEAS****, soaked overnight*
⅓ cup (70g) ***QUINOA***
½ tsp ***GROUND CUMIN***
1 tsp ***PAPRIKA***
½ cup (125ml) ***OLIVE OIL***
½ large ***EGGPLANT****, chopped into 2cm pieces*
2 medium ***CARROTS****, peeled, sliced on a diagonal*
½ bulb ***GARLIC****, cloves removed and peeled*
SALT *and freshly* ***GROUND BLACK PEPPER***
125g ***FETA****, cut into cubes*
1 large handful of ***FRESH ROCKET LEAVES***
2 fresh ***CORN COBS****, cooked and kernels sliced off*
100g ***CHERRY TOMATOES****, halved*
1 cup of ***FRESH MINT LEAVES****, roughly chopped*
1 cup ***FRESH ITALIAN PARSLEY****, roughly chopped*
1 cup ***FRESH CORIANDER LEAVES****, roughly chopped*
½ cup ***SMOKED PAPRIKA*** *dressing (see pg 202)*

Preheat oven to 180°C.

Cook the chickpeas (see pg 210) and quinoa (see pg 211).

In a large roasting dish, combine the cumin, paprika and a generous amount of olive oil then toss the eggplant pieces until well coated. Add the carrots and whole cloves of garlic, season with salt and pepper and toss to combine. Cook for 25-30 minutes or until golden brown and tender. Remove and leave to cool.

Once all ingredients have cooled, transfer to a large serving bowl. Add the remaining ingredients and toss well to mix.

Season to taste with salt and pepper.

PEARL BARLEY, EGGPLANT, POMEGRANATE & MINT SALAD

This recipe has got a lot going for it, just like Tina Brown, who kindly made it for us at Ripe. It's always a pleasure to see Tina's happy smiling face when you walk through the door in the morning.

This salad is delicious served with slow roasted lamb.

Serves 6

1¾ cups (350g) **PEARL BARLEY**
2 **CARROTS**, peeled and cut into bite size pieces
2 tbsp **DRIED MINT**
2-3 tbsp **SUMAC**
SALT and freshly **GROUND BLACK PEPPER**
7 tbsp (100ml) **OLIVE OIL**
1 medium **EGGPLANT**, cut into bite sized pieces
OLIVE OIL for pan frying
4 cloves **GARLIC**, crushed
1 large **RED ONION**, peeled, finely diced

FRESH POMEGRANATE & MINT DRESSING

Seeds of 1 whole **POMEGRANATE**, saving some for garnish
3 tbsp **POMEGRANATE MOLASSES**
1 cup (250ml) **POMEGRANATE JUICE**
¼ cup (60ml) **OLIVE OIL**
1 tbsp **LIQUID HONEY**
1 cup **FRESH MINT LEAVES**, torn, saving some for garnish
½ cup (65g) **SUNFLOWER SEEDS**, toasted (see pg 211)

Cook the pearl barley (see pg 211).

Preheat oven to 180°C.

Toss the carrots in a bowl with the dried mint, sumac, salt, pepper and 2 tbsp of the olive oil. Mix until well coated, then spread evenly on an oven tray and cook for 30-35 minutes.

Halfway through cooking, turn the carrots to cook evenly. Once cooked through, remove from oven and set aside.

On a separate oven tray place the eggplant. Toss through the rest of the oil and roast for 30 minutes. Remove from the oven and set aside.

In a frying pan over a high heat, add a dash of olive oil. Add the crushed garlic, red onion, salt and pepper and cook until soft, approximately 5 minutes. Set aside.

In a large bowl, combine the roasted carrot, eggplant, cooked onion mixture and pearl barley. Gently mix together with half of the dressing.

Season with salt and black pepper.

Place the salad onto a serving platter, drizzling the remaining dressing over it. Sprinkle with the remaining mint leaves, pomegranate seeds and sunflower seeds.

To prepare the dressing: place in a bowl the pomegranate seeds, molasses and juice, olive oil, liquid honey and fresh mint leaves and mix well until combined.

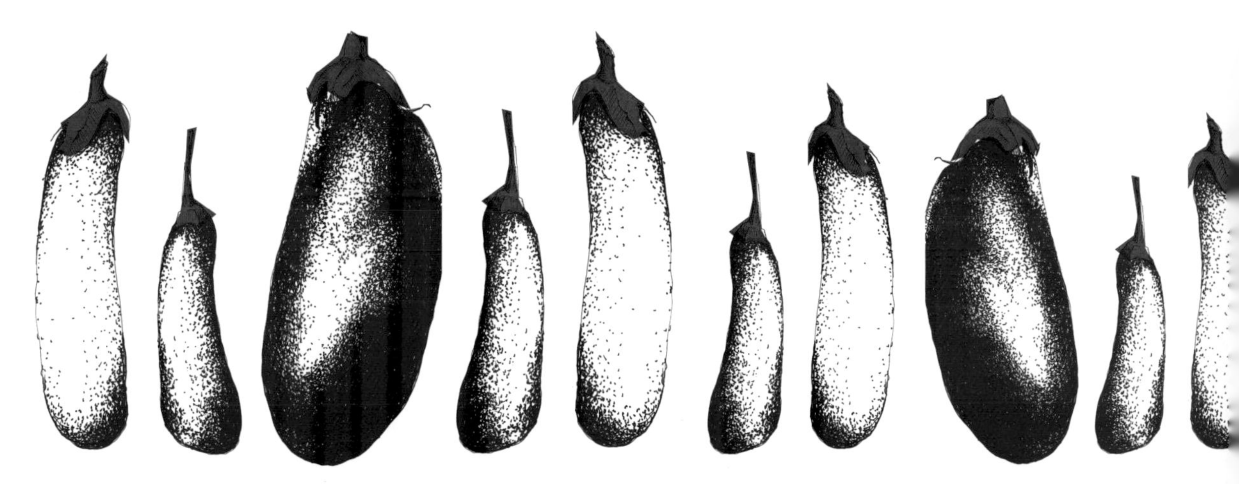

RASPBERRY & COCONUT SLICE

In this recipe raspberries can be substituted with blueberries or blackberries. The berries can be fresh or frozen – both work well.

6 ***EGG WHITES***
2 cups (320g) ***ICING SUGAR****, sieved*
2 cups (200g) fine ***DESICCATED COCONUT***
½ cup (75g) ***SELF RAISING FLOUR****, sieved*
175g ***UNSALTED BUTTER****, melted*
1½ cups (175g) ***RASPBERRIES***

Preheat oven to 180°C.

Grease and line with baking paper a 20 x 30cm slice tin. In a large bowl, mix together the egg whites, icing sugar, coconut and flour until well combined. Fold in the melted butter until just combined.

Pour mixture into the lined tin and sprinkle with berries.

Bake in oven for 35 minutes or until firm to the touch and an inserted skewer comes out clean.

Slice when cool.

CHRISTMAS BAKEWELL

A great suggestion from our neighbour Cameron Woodstock at Flotsam and Jetsam was to put a layer of fruit mince in our Bakewell Slice instead of the jam traditionally used. Both ways are good but this Christmas version is ideal to make as a festive gift for friends.

1-2 sheets (500g) frozen ***SWEET PASTRY****, or sweet pastry recipe (see pg 208)*

FRANGIPANE FILLING

200g ***GROUND ALMONDS***
200g ***UNSALTED BUTTER****, softened*
200g ***CASTER SUGAR***
4 ***EGGS***
1 cup (200g) ***CHRISTMAS FRUIT MINCE***

LEMON ICING

1 tbsp ***UNSALTED BUTTER****, melted*
1½ cups (240g) ***ICING SUGAR****, sifted*
JUICE *of 2* ***LEMONS***
RED *and* ***GREEN GLACÉ CHERRIES*** *to garnish*

Preheat oven to 180°C.

Grease a 20 x 30cm slice tin and line with baking paper.

Line the tin with a single layer of pastry and press to fit. Trim the edges to remove excess pastry and prick all over with a fork. Blind bake the pastry base in oven for 15-20 minutes (see pg 208). Remove from the oven and set aside to cool.

To prepare the frangipane filling: in a large bowl, cream together the ground almonds, butter and sugar. Add eggs one at a time, mixing well between each addition. Keep mixing for a couple of minutes until the frangipane is light in texture and pale in colour.

Spread the prepared Christmas mince over the blind baked pastry with a spatula, then spread over the frangipane. Bake for 30 minutes or until a skewer pushed in the centre comes out clean.

To prepare icing: in another bowl, combine the melted butter, icing sugar and lemon juice. Mix until smooth and thick but wet enough to be spread over the slice. Add water drop by drop if required to loosen icing.

Once cool, ice the slice and decorate with chopped red and green glacé cherries for a very festive look.

BLACK FOREST ROULADE

This roulade is inspired by the Black Forest Gateaux. It is worth the effort of removing the stones from the cherries. We don't want to be responsible for cracked teeth!

Fresh strawberries are equally delicious as an alternative to the cherries for the filling.

Serves 8-10

SPONGE

9 **EGGS**, separated
½ tsp **CREAM OF TARTAR**
2 tbsp **ICING SUGAR**
3 tsp **VANILLA EXTRACT**
225g **ICING SUGAR**
A pinch of **SALT**
50g **GROUND ALMONDS**
30g (¼ cup) **CORNFLOUR**
25g (3 tbsp) plain **FLOUR**
50g (½ cup) **COCOA POWDER**

CHERRY FILLING

1 tbsp **CORNFLOUR**
½ cup (125ml) of **JUICE**, eg. **POMEGRANATE** or **CRANBERRY**
2 tbsp **LEMON JUICE**
½ cup (110g) **CASTER SUGAR**
500g **FRESH CHERRIES**, stones removed

CREAM FILLING

300ml **CREAM**
1 tbsp **ICING SUGAR**
1 tsp **VANILLA EXTRACT**

GANACHE

200g **DARK BITTER CHOCOLATE**
60ml (¼ cup) **CREAM**
3 tbsp **KIRSCH** or cherry brandy
ICING SUGAR or cocoa to dust before serving

Preheat oven to 180°C.

Grease and line a sponge roll tin approximately 25 x 38cm with baking paper.

To prepare the sponge: beat the egg whites in a dry metal bowl with the cream of tartar and icing sugar until stiff peaks form.

In a large metal bowl place the egg yolks and vanilla extract. Whisk together with the second measure of icing sugar. Continue whisking until the yolks are pale and fluffy, approximately 5 minutes.

Into another bowl sift together the dry ingredients: salt, ground almonds, cornflour, plain flour and cocoa powder.

Using a large metal spoon, fold into the whisked yolks half of the dry ingredients and 3 tablespoons of the whisked whites. Then gently fold in the rest of the whites and the dry ingredients.

Pour the mixture into the prepared tin. Use a spatula to gently spread it evenly. Bake for 12-15 minutes until it is springy to touch. Remove from oven and set aside to cool for a few minutes. Cover with a piece of baking paper that is slightly longer than the tin.

Flip over and remove the tin so that the sponge is now between two layers of baking paper. Gently roll the sponge from the narrowest end of the tin into a log shape, and set aside and cool.

To prepare the cherry filling: dissolve the cornflour in a little of the juice.

Into a saucepan, combine all the juices, the dissolved cornflour, sugar, cherries and keep over a medium heat. Bring to the boil. Once boiling, reduce the heat to a simmer for 10 minutes or until the cherry syrup has thickened.

Remove from the heat, pour into a bowl, allow to cool.

To prepare the cream filling: place the cream, icing sugar and vanilla in a clean, dry bowl and whip together until stiff. Keep chilled.

"If at first you don't succeed, try and try again."
– Edgehill College, Bideford, Devon (my school motto)

To prepare the ganache: chop the chocolate into small pieces and place it in a microwavable bowl with the cream. Microwave on high (100%) for 40 seconds or until the chocolate has melted. You can also use the stove top method (see pg 207).

Stir with a spatula until the cream and chocolate are combined. Add the Kirsch or brandy and stir again.

If the ganache is stiff or seizing, add a tablespoon more of cream and microwave for 10 seconds. Stir again. Set aside.

To assemble: carefully unroll the sponge. Don't try and flatten it out, just gently uncurl it. Peel off the paper that the sponge was baked on. Gently spoon some of the cream filling into the most tightly curled part of the sponge. Spread about half of the cream onto the rest of the sponge, leaving 3cm at the very end without cream on it. Save other half for serving.

Dollop the cherry mixture randomly over the cream, keeping a quarter of it aside for the top.

Gently roll the filled sponge back together and transfer it to a serving platter.

Pour the ganache and the remaining cherry filling across the top of the roll. Dust with icing sugar or cocoa and serve with whipped cream.

PEACH MELBA MILLE FEUILLE

Peach Melba is a famous dessert created by Georges Auguste Escoffier while he was chef at The Savoy, London. From that, we have taken the combination of raspberry and peaches to layer this mille feuille (literally, "a thousand leaves"). This dessert can't be made in advance, it needs to be layered and enjoyed immediately.

Serves 4-6

1 ***VANILLA POD*** *cut in half lengthways*
6 ***FRESH PEACHES****, peeled and sliced or 2 x 410g canned sliced peaches in syrup*
500g ***RASPBERRIES****, fresh or thawed from frozen*
2 sheets (500g) ***BUTTER PUFF PASTRY****, thawed*
300ml ***CREAM***
1-2 tbsp ***ICING SUGAR*** *for raspberries (if needed)*
ICING SUGAR *for dusting*

SUGAR SYRUP

2 cups (440g) ***CASTER SUGAR***
2 cups (500ml) ***WATER***

Preheat oven to 200°C.

If using fresh peaches prepare the sugar syrup: place a saucepan over a medium heat and combine the sugar and water with the vanilla pod. Bring to the boil and lower the heat to a simmer until the sugar has dissolved. Poach the sliced fresh peaches in the syrup on a low heat for 5-10 minutes or until they soften but keep their shape.

If you are using canned peaches, put contents of the 2 cans in a saucepan along with the vanilla pod. Simmer on a low heat for 5 minutes, just long enough to infuse the peaches with the vanilla flavour. Again you do not want the peaches to lose their shape.

Take off the heat, remove the peaches and reserve the syrup. Add the raspberries to the reserved syrup and let them rest in the liquid until required for the assembly.

Cut each pastry sheet in half and prick each sheet all over with a fork.

Place two rectangles of pastry on an oven tray lined with baking paper. Cover the pastry with another piece of baking paper. Weigh down the pastry with another baking tray on top. This process flattens the pastry whilst baking and results in a beautifully flaky crust.

You should be able to fit two rectangles of pastry side by side on one tray (remember to leave a small gap in between them). Unless you have multiple oven trays you will be required to do this stage in two batches.

Bake for 15 minutes. Allow to cool on a metal cooling rack.

Whip the cream until soft peaks form.

Strain the peaches and raspberries. Taste the raspberries and if you think they are a bit sharp add 1 tabespoon of icing sugar to sweeten them (Frozen raspberries might not be as sweet as fresh ones).

To assemble: place one rectangle of pastry on a serving plate. Spread with ⅓ of the whipped cream, ⅓ of the peaches and ⅓ of the raspberries.

Continue layering the same way, finishing with a layer of pastry.

Dust with icing sugar to serve.

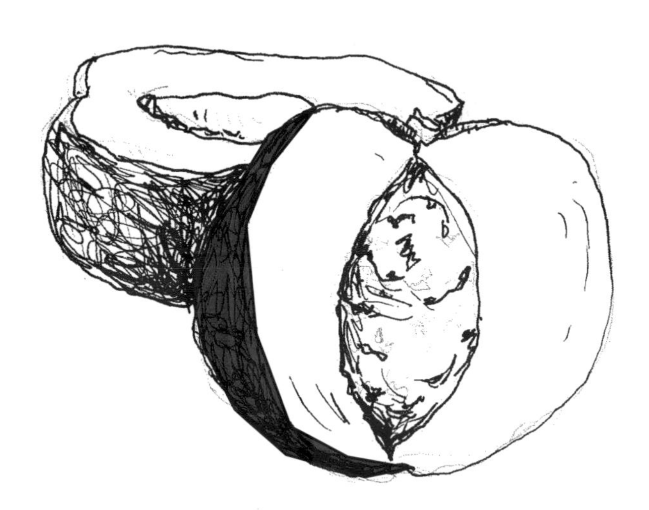

STRAWBERRY, MINT & BLACK PEPPER JAM

Makes approximately 1.75 litres

*1.25kg ripe **STRAWBERRIES***
*1.25kg **WHITE SUGAR***
JUICE** and **ZEST** of 1 **LEMON
*10 **WHOLE BLACK PEPPERCORNS**, lightly crushed*
*1 handful of **FRESH MINT LEAVES**, finely sliced*

Wash and dry the strawberries, remove stalks and cut into quarters. In a large bowl, place the strawberries in alternate layers with the sugar.

Combine the lemon juice, zest and peppercorns and pour over the strawberries. Cover and leave for 30 minutes to marinate.

Pour the contents of the bowl into a large saucepan and bring to the boil for 40 minutes. Finally add the mint leaves.

The jam is ready when the mixture has thickened a little. Drop spoonfuls onto a saucer to check the setting point (see pg 209).

Pour the hot jam into sterilised jars and seal (see pg 209).

BERRY & GIN JAM

Blackberries or raspberries are ideal for this jam. Frozen berries work equally well if you can't get hold of fresh ones. This recipe can be increased – use equal parts of berries to sugar.

Makes approximately 1.5 litres

*1kg **BERRIES**, fresh or frozen*
***JUICE** of 2-3 **LEMONS** (optional)*
*¼ cup (60ml) **GIN***
*1kg **WHITE SUGAR***

Remove any stalks from the berries and soak overnight in lemon juice and gin.

In a large heavy based saucepan combine the berries and sugar. On a low to medium heat slowly bring to a boil and continue boiling for about 20 minutes. Stir occasionally to avoid sticking.

The jam is ready when the mixture has thickened a little. Drop spoonfuls onto a saucer to check the setting point (see pg 209).

Pour the hot jam into sterilised jars and seal (see pg 209).

Asian greens.
Beans. Spinach.
Gooseberries.
Cucumbers.
Eggplant. Plums.
Rocket. Snowpeas.
Figs. Tomatoes.
Spring onions.
Sweetcorn.
Avocado. Pears.
Passionfruit.
Capsicums.
Chillies. Apples.

FEBRUARY | MARCH

At this time of the year we are often found in the herb garden at the back of Ripe enjoying after work-drinks and summer snacks.

FIG, PROSCIUTTO & GOATS' CHEESE SALAD

A sight for sore eyes. This beautiful salad was put together by our head chef, Pip Wylie. It makes a great starter or lunch with your favourite sour dough. Fully ripe figs are essential.

Serves 4

*4 small handfuls of **FRESH ROCKET LEAVES** or mesclun*
*4 fresh **FIGS**, scored into quarters, leaving whole at the base*
*4 slices **PROSCIUTTO**, torn into long strips*
*100g **SOFT GOATS' CHEESE**, crumbled*
SALT** and freshly **GROUND BLACK PEPPER
*4 tsp thyme **HONEY**, or your favourite liquid local flower honey*
EXTRA VIRGIN OLIVE OIL
***EDIBLE LAVENDER** sprigs, to garnish*

This recipe can be made on one large platter (as shown in photograph) or as follows, on individual plates.

To assemble the salads: evenly distribute ¾ of the rocket leaves between four serving plates. Top with the figs, torn prosciutto, crumbled goats' cheese and lastly the remaining rocket, keeping as much height as you can.

Lightly season with salt and freshly ground black pepper.

Drizzle over honey and a little extra virgin olive oil and decorate with lavender sprigs.

Serve immediately.

GADO GADO

We love the layered look of this traditional Indonesian dressed salad and the spicy peanut sauce makes it taste so good! Use any seasonal vegetables, such as grated courgette or thinly sliced beans.

It would be delicious served with roast or poached chicken.

Serves 6

SPICY PEANUT SAUCE

1 ***ONION****, peeled, finely diced*
3 cloves ***GARLIC****, crushed or finely chopped*
2 tbsp ***FRESH GINGER****, grated*
2 FRESH CHILLIES*, seeds included, finely chopped*
1 tbsp ***WORCESTERSHIRE SAUCE***
4 tbsp ***PEANUT OIL***
1 cup (165g) ***UNSALTED PEANUTS****, toasted and roughly chopped (see pg 211)*
1 cup (250ml) ***COCONUT CREAM***
¼ cup smooth or crunchy ***PEANUT BUTTER***

SALAD

1½ cups (180g) ***EDAMAME BEANS****, frozen*
OIL *for frying*
300g firm ***TOFU****, cut into 1cm cubes*
4 cups ***SPINACH*** *leaves, finely shredded*
¼ small ***RED CABBAGE****, finely shredded*
1 CARROT*, peeled and julienned (thin batons)*
½ ***CUCUMBER****, thinly sliced*
3 EGGS*, hard boiled and cut in half*
¼ cup (35g) ***PUMPKIN SEEDS****, toasted (see pg 211)*
¼ cup (35g) ***SESAME SEEDS****, toasted (see pg 211)*

To prepare the spicy peanut sauce: place the onion, garlic, ginger, chilli, Worcestershire and peanut oil into a saucepan. Cook over a high heat for 5 minutes.

Add the peanuts, coconut cream and peanut butter. Stir until smooth and cook for another 5 minutes. If it's too thick you can add a couple of tablespoon of hot water.

Remove from the heat and set the sauce aside until required.

To prepare the salad: blanch the edamame beans in boiling water for approximately 2 minutes and refresh in iced cold water. Drain well.

In a frying pan over a medium heat, add a dash of oil. When hot add the tofu and gently fry until golden. Remove and drain on absorbent paper.

Layer the salad ingredients onto a large serving platter in the following order; spinach, red cabbage, carrot, cucumber, edamame, tofu, and eggs. Sprinkle with the toasted seeds.

Generously drizzle over the peanut satay sauce just before serving.

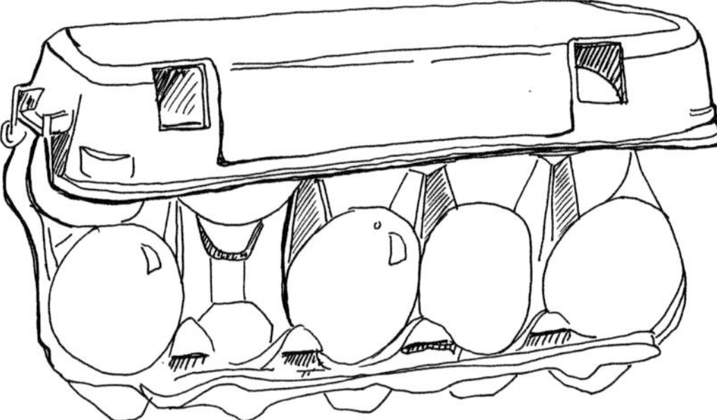

GO GO CHICKEN

My friend Megan Dunbar, "The Tupperware Queen", gave us this recipe, which is a favourite with her children, Maya and Roman. We love the fact that yoghurt has been used in the method.

Panko crumbs are a Japanese bread crumb, slightly larger than normal. This makes everything a little bit crunchier. They are available in most supermarkets.

This is delicious served with a coleslaw from The Slaw Floor (see pg 192) and mash, or a fresh Caesar salad (see pg 62).

Serves 4-6

1 cup (250ml) **UNSWEETENED NATURAL YOGHURT**
Juice of 1 **LEMON**
3 cloves **GARLIC**, crushed
1 tsp **SALT**
1 tsp freshly **GROUND BLACK PEPPER**
4-6 **CHICKEN BREASTS**, each sliced on a horizontal angle into 3 or 4 pieces
3 cups **PANKO BREAD CRUMBS**
½ cup (40g) grated **PARMESAN CHEESE**
OIL to pan fry (olive oil or grapeseed oil)

In a bowl whisk together the yoghurt, lemon juice, garlic, half the salt and half the pepper. Add the chicken to the bowl and coat well in the mixture. Cover and put in the fridge for at least an hour to marinate.

Preheat oven to 180°C.

Line an oven tray with baking paper and set aside.

Place the panko crumbs, Parmesan cheese and the rest of the salt and freshly ground black pepper into a bowl.

Remove the chicken from the fridge and place the chilled chicken fillets in the panko crumb mixture. Press the crumbs on lightly to achieve an even coating.

In a large frying pan, heat the oil over a medium to high heat. Fry the chicken on each side until the panko crumbs are a golden colour, approximately 3 minutes per side. You may need to add more oil as you go along.

Place the partly cooked chicken on an oven tray and finish cooking in the oven (approximately 10 minutes). Test the chicken by slicing through the thickest part. If cooked, the juices will run clear. Return to the oven for further cooking if juices are pink.

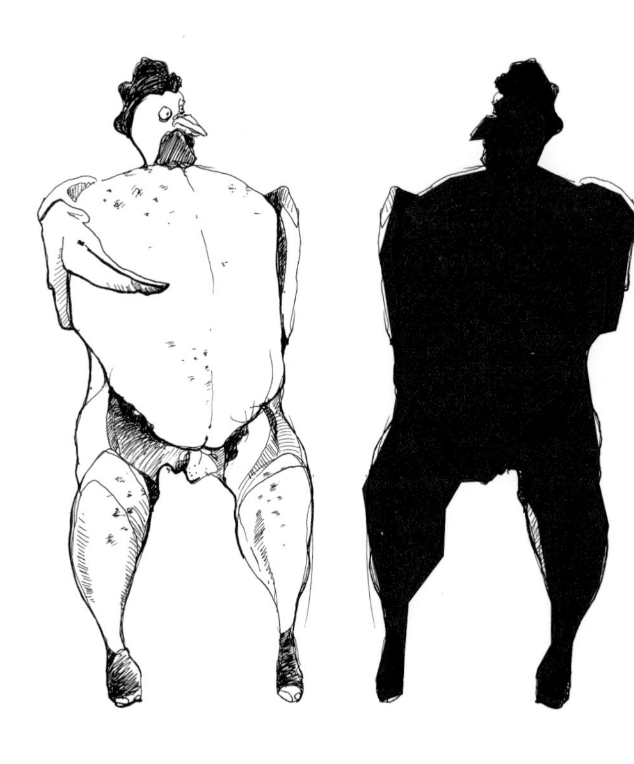

BAKED GREEN OLIVE CHICKEN

An ideal dish to complement many of the salads in this book. Alternatively, serve with a creamy polenta and some vegetables from The Green Room (see pg 162) for a delicious evening meal.

Serves 6

*6 **CHICKEN BREASTS**, skin on*
*1 whole **PRESERVED LEMON,** cut into 4 chunks*
*1 **LEMON**, sliced finely with skin on*
*1 cup (165g) large **GREEN OLIVES***
*1½ cups (375ml) **CHICKEN STOCK***
*1 tsp **SALT***
*Freshly **GROUND BLACK PEPPER***

MARINADE

*1 whole bulb **GARLIC**, peeled and roughly chopped*
*1 tsp **FENNEL SEEDS***
*1 tsp **CUMIN SEEDS***
*1 tsp **CORIANDER SEEDS***
*2 tbsp **WHITE WINE VINEGAR***
*2 tbsp **OLIVE OIL***
*½ cup (125ml) **WHITE WINE***

To prepare the marinade: combine the garlic, seeds, white wine vinegar, olive oil and white wine in a bowl.

Coat the chicken in the marinade and leave covered in the fridge for a minimum of 2 hours.

Preheat oven to 180°C.

Place a large frying pan over a high heat. Pan fry the marinated chicken for 2-3 minutes each side.

Lay the partly cooked chicken in a deep sided roasting dish with the remaining marinade, preserved lemon, sliced fresh lemon, green olives and chicken stock. Season with 1 teaspoon salt and some freshly ground black pepper. Cook for 30 minutes. Test the chicken by slicing through the thickest part. If cooked, the juices will run clear. Return to the oven for further cooking if juices are pink.

Place the chicken on a serving platter. Pour the cooking juices into a saucepan. Reduce the liquid over a high heat for 1-2 minutes or until the juices have slightly thickened. Pour the sauce over the chicken to serve.

MOUSSAKA

Ideally served with a green salad from The Greenhouse (see pg 65).

Serves 4-6

MEAT SAUCE

2 tbsp ***OLIVE OIL***
1 large ***ONION****, peeled, finely chopped*
1 stalk ***CELERY****, diced*
3 cloves ***GARLIC****, peeled and finely chopped*
1 ***CARROT****, peeled and diced*
1 tsp ***CINNAMON***
600g ***LAMB MINCE***
400g can ***CRUSHED TOMATOES***
1 tbsp ***TOMATO PUREE***
2 tbsp ***FRESH MINT LEAVES****, roughly chopped*
1 cup (250ml) ***RED WINE***
SALT *and freshly* ***GROUND BLACK PEPPER***

1 large ***EGGPLANT****, sliced thinly*
OLIVE OIL *for brushing*

BÉCHAMEL SAUCE

2 tbsp ***BUTTER***
2 tbsp plain ***FLOUR***
2½ cups (625ml) ***MILK****, gently warmed*
150g ***FETA****, crumbled*
150g ***COTTAGE CHEESE***
1 tsp ***PAPRIKA***
1 large handful of ***GRATED CHEESE***

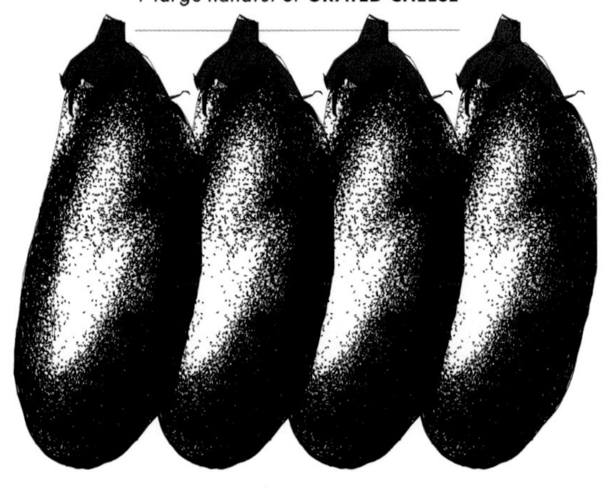

To prepare the meat sauce: in a large frying pan, heat the oil over a medium to high heat. Add the onion, celery, garlic, carrot and cinnamon. Cook for approximately 5 minutes. Add the lamb mince and sauté until brown.

Add the crushed tomatoes, tomato puree, mint and red wine and cook over a medium heat for 20 minutes. Season with salt and pepper to taste.

Preheat grill or oven to 200°C.

To prepare the eggplant: line an oven tray with a layer of baking paper and grease with a little oil. Thinly slice (5-10mm) oval rounds of eggplant. Brush both sides of the eggplant with olive oil, sprinkle with salt and place on the prepared tray. Grill or bake until golden and tender, flip over and grill on the other side, approximately 10 minutes per side.

Set aside and reduce oven temperature to 180°C.

To prepare the béchamel sauce: place a medium sized saucepan on a low to medium heat and melt the butter.

Add the flour and cook while stirring for 1 minute until it turns a gentle golden colour. Gradually add the warmed milk, stirring all the time to avoid lumps forming.

Bring the sauce to a high heat until it thickens, stirring constantly.

Over low heat add the crumbled feta and cottage cheese. Mix and heat through until just combined and season with salt and freshly ground black pepper to taste.

To assemble the moussaka: lightly grease an ovenproof deep sided 20 x 30cm dish.

Spoon half of the lamb mixture into the dish. Cover with a layer of eggplant slices and pour over half of the béchamel sauce. Repeat this process with the remaining ingredients. Season with paprika and freshly ground black pepper. Sprinkle with grated cheese.

Bake in oven for around 30 minutes or until the béchamel sauce is golden on top. Remove from oven and leave to stand for 5 minutes before serving.

RATATOUILLE

This is a great dish to make when capsicums and eggplant are cheap and plentiful. Freeze to use in the winter months. Ratatouille is fantastic served with panfried fish or lamb.

Serves 4-6

1 **RED ONION**, peeled
1 **RED CAPSICUM**, de-seeded
1 **YELLOW CAPSICUM**, de-seeded
1 medium **EGGPLANT**
3 **COURGETTES**
3 tbsp **OLIVE OIL**
3 cloves **GARLIC**, crushed
2 x 400g **CANNED TOMATOES**, chopped
1 tsp **TOMATO PASTE**
1 tsp **HONEY**
½ tsp **SALT** and freshly **GROUND BLACK PEPPER**
1 cup **FRESH BASIL LEAVES**
1 tbsp good **EXTRA VIRGIN OLIVE OIL**, for serving

Chop the onion, capsicums, eggplant and courgette into equal, large bite sized pieces.

In a large saucepan, heat the olive oil over a medium to high heat. Cook the onion and garlic until lightly golden in colour.

Add the eggplant and cook for a few more minutes. Next add the capsicums and cook for a further 5 minutes. Finally add the tomatoes, tomato paste and honey.

Cover the pan and simmer on a low to medium heat for 25 minutes. At this point stir in the courgettes. If the sauce is too thick add a dash of water. Cover the pan again and simmer on a low heat for another 20 minutes.

Lastly, mix through the fresh basil leaves and a good splash of extra virgin olive oil. Season well with salt and pepper.

RIPE CAESAR

The king of salads, ideal with Go Go Chicken (see pg 56). Freshly baked croutons are best in this salad. They are a great way of using up old bread and they store well in an air tight container.

Serves 4-6

4 slices **BREAD**
3 tbsp **OLIVE OIL**
3 rashers **STREAKY BACON**
1 large or 3 **BABY COS LETTUCES**, leaves separated and washed
4 **EGGS**, boiled and cut into wedges
3 **ANCHOVY FILLETS**, roughly chopped
1 cup **CAESAR DRESSING** (see pg 205)
½ cup (40g) **PARMESAN**, shaved
SALT and freshly **GROUND BLACK PEPPER**

Preheat oven to 110°C.

To prepare the croutons: remove the crusts from the bread and chop into 2cm cubes.

Place the bread cubes on an oven tray and drizzle with the olive oil. Season with salt and freshly ground black pepper and toss to coat.

Bake in the oven for approximately 20 minutes, or until golden brown and crunchy. Remove and set aside. Increase the oven temperature to 180°C.

Place the bacon on an oven tray and cook until crispy. Remove and set aside.

Allow the bacon to cool and then roughly chop.

To assemble the salad: in a large bowl tear the cos lettuce into bite sized pieces. Add the croutons, bacon, eggs and anchovies. Drizzle with half of the dressing and toss to coat.

Serve with the remainder of the dressing drizzled over the top of the salad or served on the side. Sprinkle with shaved Parmesan and season if needed with salt and pepper.

THE GREENHOUSE

Make the most of the abundant varieties of lettuce we have available to us now. Here are four delicious leafy salads we recommend.

ICEBERG, ORANGE & HAZELNUT

Serves 4-6

1½ medium ***ICEBERG LETTUCE****, finely shredded*
¼ cup (40g) ***HAZELNUTS****, toasted (see pg 211) and roughly chopped*
1 ***AVOCADO****, peeled and sliced*
2 ***ORANGES****, peeled and segmented*
SALT *and freshly* ***GROUND BLACK PEPPER***

DRESSING

2 tbsp ***POMEGRANATE MOLASSES***
3 tbsp ***AVOCADO OIL***
3 tbsp ***EXTRA VIRGIN OLIVE OIL***

Place dressing ingredients into a jar with a tightly fitting lid. Shake well.

Place all the salad ingredients on a platter and then pour over the dressing. Season with salt and pepper and serve.

ROCKET, RADICCHIO & PARMESAN

Serves 4-6

3 cups ***FRESH ROCKET LEAVES***
1 whole ***RADICCHIO****, thinly sliced*
½ cup (40g) ***PARMESAN****, shaved*

DRESSING

¼ cup ***BALSAMIC REDUCTION*** *(see pg 202)*
¼ cup (60ml) ***EXTRA VIRGIN OLIVE OIL***

Place dressing ingredients into a jar with a tightly fitting lid. Shake well.

Place salad leaves on a platter, sprinkle on Parmesan and drizzle on the dressing.

WITLOOF, BLUE CHEESE & VINCOTTO

Serves 4-6

4-5 ***WITLOOF****, leaves separated and thickly shredded*
150g ***CREAMY BLUE CHEESE****, crumbled*
¼ cup (60ml) ***VINCOTTO***
¼ cup (60ml) ***EXTRA VIRGIN OLIVE OIL***
Freshly ***GROUND BLACK PEPPER***

Place leaves on a platter, scatter over the blue cheese. Drizzle with vincotto and olive oil and season with black pepper.

FENNEL, WATERCRESS & POMEGRANATE

Serves 4-6

1 large or 2 small ***FENNEL BULBS****, finely sliced*
150g ***GREEN BEANS****, shredded*
100g ***WATERCRESS***
2 tbsp ***SESAME SEEDS****, toasted (see pg 211)*
SEEDS *of 1* ***POMEGRANATE***
JUICE *of 1* ***LEMON***
2 tbsp ***EXTRA VIRGIN OLIVE OIL***
SEA SALT FLAKES
Freshly ***GROUND BLACK PEPPER***

Place salad ingredients and seeds on a platter. Squeeze over the lemon, drizzle over the olive oil and season with salt and pepper.

MIDDLE EASTERN TABOULEH WITH LABNE

Have some fun making the labne, a traditional Middle Eastern cheese which is made from strained yoghurt.

Use the labne as part of antipasto, in salads or spread on crostini. The tabouleh is also great without it, and a good replacement would be feta, although the labne is well worth the effort!

Labne needs to be made 24-36 hours before it is required.

Serves 4-6

LABNE

500g ***GREEK YOGHURT***

1 tbsp ***SALT***

1 tsp ***PAPRIKA***

1 tbsp ***EXTRA VIRGIN OLIVE OIL***

DRESSING

¾ cup (180ml) ***OLIVE OIL***

1 tsp ***HONEY***

2 cloves ***GARLIC****, crushed*

¼ cup ***FRESH MINT LEAVES****, finely chopped*

SALT *and freshly* ***GROUND BLACK PEPPER***

LABNE BALLS

1 cup of prepared ***LABNE***

2 tsp ***CORIANDER SEEDS****, toasted (see pg 211)*

2 tsp ***FENNEL SEEDS****, toasted (see pg 211)*

1 tsp ***CUMIN SEEDS****, toasted (see pg 211)*

TABOULEH

1 cup (200g) ***BULGHUR WHEAT,***

Seeds of 1 or 2 ***POMEGRANATE***

1 medium ***RED ONION****, peeled. finely chopped*

3 cups ***FRESH CURLY PARSLEY****, roughly chopped*

½ cup ***FRESH MINT LEAVES****, roughly chopped*

1 x 250g punnet of ***CHERRY TOMATOES****, halved*

JUICE *and* ***ZEST*** *of 2* ***LEMONS***

To prepare the labne: use a new clean cheese/chux cloth (approximately 40 x 40cm) and a clean sieve. Make sure to run the clean cloth under cold water and then wring it out once you're ready to use it.

Rest the sieve over a bowl and line it with the wet cloth, ensuring the corners are overhanging the edges.

Stir the salt into the yoghurt and pour into the lined seive. Fold the corners of the cloth up over the mix.

Place cans on top to weigh down the cloth and assist in straining. Leave in the fridge for at least 24 hours.

Remove the cans and unfold the cloth.

Place a plate over the sieve and flip the labne out onto the plate.

To prepare the tabouleh: soak the bulghur wheat (see pg 210) and strain well.

To prepare the dressing: place all the ingredients in a bowl and mix well until combined.

To prepare the labne balls: place the mixed toasted seeds on a plate. Rub a little oil on your hands and roll teaspoonfuls of labne lightly into balls then turn the balls in the seed mixture to coat lightly.

To prepare the salad: transfer the bulghur wheat into a bowl and add all of the remaining ingredients except the labne. Add the dressing and stir well to combine. Season to taste with salt and pepper.

Pile the tabouleh onto a serving platter and scatter the labne balls on the top.

CHILLI PRAWN SPAGHETTI

This can be served hot or cold. Serve with a fresh salad from The Green Room.

Serves 4

250g dried **SPAGHETTI**
¼ cup **OLIVE OIL**
8 cloves **GARLIC**, peeled and finely sliced
2 fresh **RED CHILLIES**, finely sliced with seeds removed if a milder taste is preferred, or ½-1 tsp chilli flakes
25g **BUTTER**
200g **FRESH PRAWNS**, tail on
1 x 250g punnet of **CHERRY TOMATOES**, halved
JUICE and **ZEST** of 1 **LEMON**
½ whole **PRESERVED LEMON**, finely chopped (optional)
SALT and freshly **GROUND BLACK PEPPER**
1 **AVOCADO**, skin and stone removed, cut into bite sized wedges
½ cup **FRESH ITALIAN PARSLEY**, roughly chopped

Cook the spaghetti as per the instructions on the packet and set aside to cool if serving salad cold.

Place the olive oil in a frying pan over a high heat and add the garlic and chilli. Cook for 1 minute taking care not to burn the garlic.

Add the butter and prawns. Cook until they have changed colour. Remove from the heat.

In a large serving bowl place the cooked prawns, spaghetti, cherry tomatoes, lemon juice, lemon zest and preserved lemon. Toss well to combine and season to taste with salt and pepper.

Add the avocado wedges, toss through gently. Sprinkle over the parsley and serve.

CRUNCHY QUINOA & KIDNEY BEAN SALAD

This is a raw vegetable salad packed with flavour and goodness. Delicious with the addition of tuna.

Serves 4-6

⅔ cup (120g) **QUINOA**
½ cup (100g) **KIDNEY BEANS**, soaked overnight
2 **CARROTS**, peeled and diced finely
1 medium **RED ONION**, peeled, diced finely
3 **COURGETTES**, diced finely
1 **RED CAPSICUM**, de-seeded and diced finely
1 **YELLOW CAPSICUM**, de-seeded and diced finely
1 handful of **CHERRY TOMATOES**, halved
JUICE and **ZEST** of 1 **LEMON**
1 cup **FRESH ITALIAN PARSLEY**, finely chopped
½ cup **FRESH DILL**, finely chopped
¼ cup **FRESH MINT LEAVES**, finely chopped
1 cup **DILL** or mint dressing (see pg 202)
SALT and freshly **GROUND BLACK PEPPER**

Cook the quinoa (see pg 211) and kidney beans (see pg 210).

Place all of the ingredients in a large serving bowl and stir to combine. Season with salt and pepper and serve.

"No man is lonely while eating spaghetti; it requires so much attention." – Christopher Morley

SPICED EGGPLANT & PEANUT SALAD

Andrea Saunders says that this is one of her favourite salads that she has created in the Ripe kitchen. The pungent spices with the sweet eggplant and peanuts makes this a fabulous accompaniment to BBQ lamb.

Serves 4-6

1 tsp ***CORIANDER SEEDS****, toasted (see pg 211)*
1 tsp ***CUMIN SEEDS****, toasted*
1 tsp ***SMOKED PAPRIKA***
1 tbsp ***CURRY POWDER***
1 tsp ***DRIED CHILLI FLAKES***
1 tsp ***GROUND CUMIN***
½ tsp ***SALT***
2 cloves ***GARLIC****, crushed*
¼ cup (60ml) ***OLIVE OIL***
2 medium sized ***EGGPLANT****, cut in 2cm cubes*
SALT *and freshly* ***GROUND BLACK PEPPER***
2 handfuls of ***BABY SPINACH****, washed*
1-2 cups ***YOGHURT DRESSING*** *(see pg 204)*
1 cup ***FRESH CORIANDER LEAVES****, roughly chopped with a few leaves set aside for garnish*
¾ cup (125g) ***ROASTED UNSALTED PEANUTS****, roughly chopped*
JUICE *of 1* ***LEMON***

Preheat oven to 200°C.

With a mortar and pestle, crush together the toasted seeds, smoked paprika, curry powder, chilli flakes, ground cumin and salt. Tip into a large bowl. Add the crushed garlic, oil and the eggplant pieces. Mix well to coat.

Place the seasoned eggplant on an oven tray lined with baking paper and roast for approximately 30 minutes, turning once. Roast until tender and beginning to brown.

Allow to cool. Season to taste with salt and pepper.

To assemble the salad: on a large platter layer half of the spiced eggplant, spinach leaves, a drizzle of yoghurt dressing, fresh coriander leaves and some peanuts. Repeat the sequence with the remaining ingredients and finish with fresh coriander leaves. Finally, add a good squeeze of lemon juice and a drizzle of the remaining dressing.

FRESH CORN & GREEN BEAN SALAD

At Ripe we still think the best and easiest way to eat corn is hot on the cob with lashings of butter. Coming in a close second however is cooking the corn and slicing off the kernels to add to a simple salad, like this one here.

2 ***FENNEL BULBS****, roots trimmed*
1 tbsp soft ***BROWN SUGAR*** *or liquid honey*
JUICE *and* ***ZEST*** *of 2* ***LEMONS***
4 fresh ***CORN COBS***
500g ***GREEN BEANS****, topped and tailed*
1 cup (165g) ***KALAMATA OLIVES***
250g punnet of ***CHERRY TOMATOES****, halved*
1 cup ***FRESH ITALIAN PARSLEY****, roughly chopped*
1 cup ***BASIL DRESSING*** *(see pg 203)*
SALT *and freshly* ***GROUND BLACK PEPPER***

Thinly slice the fennel and place in a bowl with the brown sugar and lemon juice. Allow to marinate for 20 minutes.

In a large saucepan pour in enough water to cover the corn cobs. Bring to the boil and cook until the cobs are tender, approximately 10 minutes. Remove from the water. Reserve the water and keep it on the heat.

In the boiling water blanch the trimmed beans for 2 minutes then remove and refresh in iced cold water.

When cool enough cut the kernels of corn off the cob.

On a large serving platter layer up the fennel, corn, beans, olives, cherry tomatoes and parsley. Drizzle over the basil dressing. Season with salt and pepper.

GINGERBREAD & STEWED FIGS

175g ***UNSALTED BUTTER****, cut into small pieces*
1 cup (250ml) ***WATER***
⅓ cup (120g) ***TREACLE***
⅔ cup (230g) ***GOLDEN SYRUP***
2 ***EGGS***
1⅓ cups (220g) soft ***BROWN SUGAR***
2 tsp ***BAKING SODA***
2 tsp ***GROUND GINGER***
2 tsp ***GROUND CINNAMON***
2⅓ cups (265g) plain ***FLOUR***

Preheat oven to 180°C.

Grease and line a loaf tin, approximately 12 x 22 x 7cm in size.

Combine in a saucepan the butter, water, treacle and golden syrup. Heat and stir until the butter has melted and then remove from the heat.

In a mixing bowl whisk the eggs and sugar until combined. Add the melted butter mixture and whisk until smooth.

Sift together all dry ingredients. Add to wet mixture, whisking together until smooth. The mix will be very wet in consistency. Pour into the prepared tin and bake for 1 hour or until a skewer inserted into the centre comes out clean.

Serve with stewed figs or just slathered with butter!

STEWED FIGS

12 fresh ***FIGS*** *chopped in half*
JUICE *and* ***ZEST*** *of 3* ***ORANGES***
1 ***CINNAMON STICK***
2 whole ***STAR ANISE***
¼ cup (50g) ***MUSCOVADO*** *or soft brown sugar*

Place all ingredients in a saucepan and simmer on a low heat for 15 minutes. Add a little water if needed to prevent from boiling dry.

ALMOND PEARS

Charlotte Drayton, who was a great baker at Ripe, shaped these little beauties for us. As well as being so cute they are wheat, gluten and dairy free.

Makes around 15

200g ***CASTER SUGAR***
2 ***EGG WHITES***
1 tsp ***GROUND CARDAMOM***
150g ***GROUND ALMONDS***
50g ***GROUND PISTACHIO***
ROSE WATER
15 ***WHOLE CLOVES***

Preheat oven to 170°C.

In a large bowl whisk together the sugar and egg whites. Add cardamom and ground nuts and stir with a spoon until thick and quite firm.

Sprinkle a little rose water on your hands then roll tablespoonfuls of mixture into large walnut sized balls.

Pinch the top of the ball to make a pear shape.

Use the clove to poke in the top of the 'pear'. It will look like a stalk.

Place the "pears" on an oven tray lined with baking paper and bake for 15-20 minutes, or until golden.

ROCKO SLICE

A chocoholics delight.

300g ***SUPER WINE BISCUITS****, ground into crumbs*
⅓ cup (50g) plain ***FLOUR***
½ cup (50g) ***COCOA***
¾ cup (90g) ***DESICCATED COCONUT***
300g ***UNSALTED BUTTER****, melted*
1 x 395g tin ***SWEETENED CONDENSED MILK***
½ cup (80g) soft ***BROWN SUGAR***
100g ***UNSALTED BUTTER***
3 tbsp (75g) ***GOLDEN SYRUP***

TOPPING

200g ***DARK CHOCOLATE****, melted (see pg 207)*
1 tbsp ***VEGETABLE OIL***

Preheat oven to 180°C and move the oven rack to the top position.

Grease a 20 x 30cm slice tin and line with baking paper.

In a large bowl, combine the biscuit crumbs, flour, cocoa, coconut and melted butter until well incorporated.

Empty this into the slice tin and press with the back of a metal spoon to flatten. Cover and refrigerate.

In a saucepan over a low to medium heat, combine the condensed milk, brown sugar, butter and golden syrup. Stir constantly with a wooden spoon as this mixture catches easily. Mix until thickened.

Pour over the chilled base. Bake on the top rack for approximately 20 minutes or until the caramel has bubbled and browned.

Chill completely before icing.

To prepare the topping: melt the chocolate and oil together (see pg 207). Pour carefully over the chilled caramel, smoothing with a spatula.

Refrigerate until chocolate has set and slice.

CHOCOLATE NESTS

Kids love making these. Nikau Gardner has given his lick of approval. Fill the nests with any type of little lollies. Very popular at children's parties.

Makes 12

4 cups (100g) ***COCOA POPS*** *or a similar chocolate rice cereal*
300g ***DARK CHOCOLATE****, melted (see pg 207)*
1 cup (70g) ***LONG THREAD COCONUT***
CANDY COATED EGGS

Line a 12 hole standard muffin tray with paper cases or lightly grease.

In a large bowl, mix together the Cocoa Pops, melted chocolate and coconut until all the ingredients are well coated with the chocolate.

Spoon into the muffin cups and, using the back of a wet metal spoon, flatten the centre to create a nest shape.

Refrigerate until set, then fill the hollow with your choice of little lollies.

HONEY CRACKLES

Work carefully with this mixture, as the toffee sets quickly and is very hot.

225g ***UNSALTED BUTTER***
⅔ cup (150g) ***CASTER SUGAR***
2 tbsp ***RUNNY HONEY***
5 cups (125g) ***RICE BUBBLES*** *or a similar puffed rice cereal*

Grease and line a 20 x 30cm slice tray with baking paper or line a 12 hole muffin tray with paper cases, depending on the final shape you are after.

In a saucepan, combine the butter, sugar, and honey. Place over a medium heat and bring to the boil.

Continue to boil for 5-10 minutes, or until a teaspoonful of the mixture dropped into a glass of cold water forms a soft ball that can be rolled between your fingertips.

Place the Rice Bubbles in a large bowl and pour the hot honey mixture over. Mix quickly with a wooden spoon. Spoon immediately into muffin cups or press into the lined slice tray. Cover and refrigerate until hard.

Nikau Gardner

FIG & ORANGE TART

A classic taste combination. It's essential to use figs when they are at their ripest.

Serves 8-10

1-2 sheets frozen ***SWEET PASTRY,***
or Sweet pastry recipe *(see pg 208)*

FILLING

½ cup (80g) soft ***BROWN SUGAR***
50g ***UNSALTED BUTTER***
12 ***FIGS****, fresh, halved*
2 whole ***STAR ANISE***
2 ***ORANGES****,* ***ZEST*** *and* ***JUICE*** *from one, the other thinly sliced, skin and all.*

FRANGIPANE

200g ***GROUND ALMONDS***
200g ***CASTER SUGAR***
200g ***BUTTER****, softened*
4 ***EGGS***

Preheat oven to 180°C.

Line a 26cm fluted tart tin with sweet pastry and chill while you make the filling.

To prepare the filling: in a medium saucepan over a medium heat, melt the brown sugar and butter together. Cook until sugar has dissolved. Add the halved figs, star anise, orange zest and juice.

Poach until figs have softened, approximately 10 minutes. Add the orange slices after 5 minutes.

Remove from the heat and set aside.

To prepare the frangipane: in the bowl of an electric mixer, beat the almonds, caster sugar and butter on high speed until they are pale, creamy and light in texture.

Add the eggs one at a time, scraping down the sides of the bowl and beating well after each addition.

Pile into the tart shell. Spread evenly with a spatula and top with three quarters of the fig and orange mixture.

Bake for 40 minutes until the frangipane is golden in colour and firm to the touch.

Remove from the oven and allow to cool.

Before serving, carefully remove the tart from the tin and transfer it to a serving plate. Top it with the remainder of the fig and orange mixture and serve with cinnamon cream (see pg 208) or ice cream.

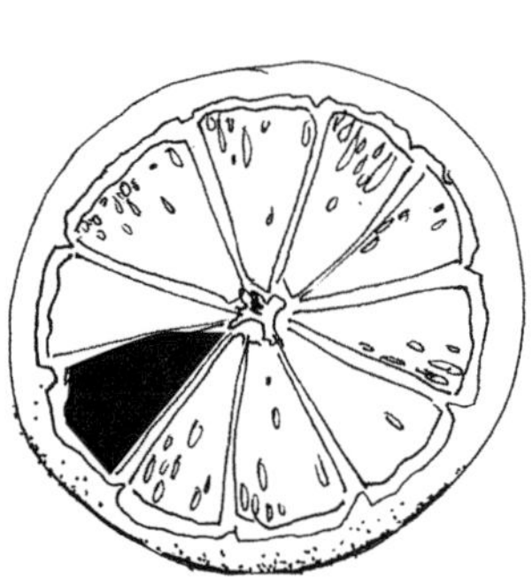

PASSIONATE CHEESECAKE

By all means change the topping to a seasonal fruit coulis of your choice if you can't get a hold of fresh passion fruit. In the winter months tinned cherries also make a delicious alternative.

Serves 10-12

BASE

250g ***SUPER WINE BISCUITS***
100g ***UNSALTED BUTTER****, melted*

FILLING

½ cup (125ml) boiling ***WATER***
1 tbsp ***POWDERED GELATINE***
500g ***CREAM CHEESE****, softened*
½ cup (110g) ***CASTER SUGAR***
8 ***FRESH PASSION FRUIT****, pulp*
500ml ***CREAM***

TOPPING

8 ***PASSION FRUIT****, pulp*
1 tsp ***ICING SUGAR***

To prepare the base: line a 26cm spring form tin with baking paper. Crush the biscuits using a plastic bag and rolling pin or process the biscuits to a crumb in a food processor. Add the melted butter and combine. Spoon the biscuit mix into tin. Smooth and flatten down with the back of a spoon. Cover and keep refrigerated until required.

To prepare the filling: pour the boiling water into a microwave proof bowl. Sprinkle over the gelatine and microwave on high for 30-40 seconds or until the gelatine has dissolved.

In a food processor or large mixing bowl place the cream cheese, caster sugar and passion fruit pulp. Blend until smooth. Add the gelatine mix and pulse for approximately 20 seconds, until the gelatine is completely incorporated.

In another bowl whip the cream until soft peaks have formed. Fold the cream cheese mixture gently into the whipped cream and pour onto the prepared biscuit base. Smooth the top gently with a spatula.

Cover and refrigerate overnight to set.

To prepare the topping: mix passion fruit pulp and icing sugar. Taste to see if sweet enough – otherwise add a little more icing sugar. Drizzle over cheesecake.

When ready to serve, run a warmed knife around the edge of the cheesecake to release it from the tin and remove.

TOMATO KASUNDI

Makes approximately 3 litres

2 tbsp **BLACK MUSTARD SEEDS**
2 cups (500ml) **MALT VINEGAR**
2½ kg ripe **TOMATOES**
250g **FRESH GINGER**, peeled and roughly chopped
20 cloves **GARLIC**, peeled
2 tbsp (30ml) **VEGETABLE OIL**
2 tbsp **GROUND TURMERIC**
4 tbsp **GROUND CUMIN**
2 tbsp **CHILLI POWDER**
10-15 fresh mild large **RED CHILLIES**, halved, seeds removed, roughly chopped
1½ cups (330g) **WHITE SUGAR**
1½ tbsp **SALT**

Soak mustard seeds in the vinegar overnight.

Mark the tomatoes with an "X" on the base and plunge into boiling water for 30 seconds. Transfer immediately into a bowl of iced water. Drain the tomatoes, peel and chop. Set aside.

Purée the ginger and garlic in a food processor until smooth. Add the tomatoes and blend for another minute.

Heat the oil in a large saucepan until smoking. Remove from heat and add turmeric, cumin and chilli powder, stirring continuously.

Place the saucepan back on a medium heat. Add the soaked mustard seeds, vinegar, puréed tomato mixture, fresh chilli, sugar and salt. Simmer for approximately one hour or until the mixture becomes pulpy.

Spoon into heated, sterilised jars and seal while hot (see pg 209 for bottling tips). Allow a week before using to intensify and develop the flavours.

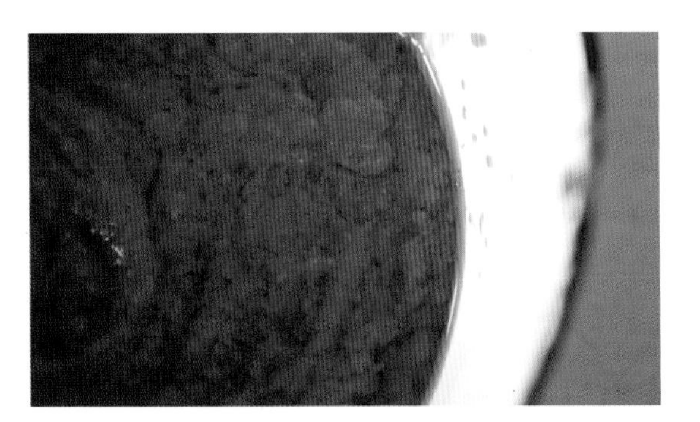

SPICY TOMATO RELISH

Makes approximately 3 litres

3kg ripe **TOMATOES**, roughly chopped
1kg **ONIONS**, peeled and roughly chopped
2 tbsp **SALT**
2 cups (500ml) **MALT VINEGAR**
1kg **WHITE SUGAR**
4-6 small **CHILLIES**, finely chopped
3 tbsp **CORNFLOUR**
3 tbsp **CURRY POWDER**
2 tsp **MUSTARD POWDER**
1 cup (250ml) **WATER**

Place the tomatoes and onions in a bowl. Sprinkle with the salt and leave overnight.

Once soaked, pour off the liquid. Place the tomatoes and onions into a large saucepan. Add the vinegar, sugar and chillies. Gently simmer for 30 minutes.

Combine the cornflour, curry and mustard powder with the water and mix to make a paste.

Gradually stir the paste into the cooking mixture and continue to boil. Constantly stir the relish until it thickens.

Spoon into heated, sterilised jars and seal while hot (see pg 209 for bottling tips).

SPICY PLUM SAUCE

1kg ***PLUMS****, de-stoned and roughly chopped*
2 cups (320g) soft ***BROWN SUGAR***
1 bulb ***GARLIC****, peeled and crushed*
1 tbsp ***GROUND GINGER***
1 tbsp ***FRESH GINGER****, peeled and grated*
1 tsp freshly ***GROUND BLACK PEPPER***
1 tbsp ***SALT***
2 cups (320g) ***SULTANAS***
½ cup (125ml) ***BALSAMIC VINEGAR***
1½ cups (375ml) ***WATER***

Place all of the ingredients into a large heavy based saucepan and bring to the boil. Once boiling, reduce the heat to a simmer for 30 minutes.

Blend with a stick blender to a smooth consistency. Taste and season if needed. Pour the sauce into sterilised bottles (see pg 209 for bottling tips) and seal.

CAPSICUM JAM

1kg ***RED CAPSICUMS***
A drizzle of ***VEGETABLE OIL***
½ cup (125ml) ***WHITE WINE VINEGAR***
2 cups (450g) ***WHITE SUGAR***
JUICE *and* ***ZEST*** *of 1* ***LEMON***
1 tsp ***DRIED CHILLI FLAKES***
1 tsp ***SMOKED PAPRIKA***

Preheat oven to 180°C.

Place the capsicums on a baking paper lined tray, drizzle with the oil and distribute evenly. Place tray in the oven and, turning occasionally, roast for approximately 40 minutes.

Remove the capsicums from the oven and set aside in a bowl covered with plastic. Let them cool completely. Peel the blistered capsicums, removing the skin, membranes and seeds. Place the flesh in a food processor and blend until smooth.

Transfer the capsicums to a large saucepan over a low heat. Add the vinegar, sugar, lemon zest and juice, stirring to combine. Stir until the sugar dissolves. Add the chilli flakes and smoked paprika.

Increase the heat and boil for 15 minutes, stirring occasionally. Check that the jam has reached setting point by placing a drop onto a ceramic saucer and pushing with your finger to see if the jam wrinkles. If it does, remove from the heat and wait until bubbles subside.

Remove with a metal spoon any froth that has settled on the surface. Spoon the hot jam into heated, sterilised jars, (see pg 209 for bottling tips) seal and set aside to cool.

Quince.Guavas.
Tamarillos.Leeks.
Squash.Apples.
Pears.Pumpkin.
Mushrooms.
Courgette.Onion.
Spinach.Beetroot.
Broccoli.Celery.
Feijoas.Grapes.
Kale.Kiwi fruit.
Radicchio.
Rhubarb.Radish.
Silverbeet.Turnip.

APRIL | MAY

A tamarillo and feijoa frenzy.

CARAMELISED ONION & LENTIL SOUP

Serves 4-6

3 whole bulbs **GARLIC**
4 tbsp **OLIVE OIL**
6 **RED ONIONS**, *peeled and thinly sliced*
2 ltrs (8 cups) **CHICKEN STOCK**
1 cup (225g) **GREEN PUY LENTILS**
2 **FRESH BAY LEAVES**
SALT *and freshly* **GROUND BLACK PEPPER**
½ cup **FRESH ITALIAN PARSLEY**, *finely chopped*

Preheat oven to 160°C.

To roast the bulbs of garlic, trim off the top leaving the bulb whole and the skin on.

Place the garlic in a foil lined baking dish and drizzle half the oil over the bulbs.

Bake for 35 minutes then allow to cool.

With the blunt side of a knife, squeeze out each clove of garlic and discard the skins.

Heat the remaining oil in a large saucepan over a low to medium heat. Add the onions and cook for 30 minutes or until soft and caramelised. Add the stock, lentils, roasted garlic and bay leaves.

Bring to the boil. Lower the heat to a simmer for 20 minutes.

Taste and season with salt and pepper. Sprinkle with fresh parsley and serve with crusty bread, fresh croutons or cheesy scones (see pg 120).

SMOKED BACON & GREEN SPLIT PEA SOUP

Serves 4-6

1½ cups (300g) **GREEN SPLIT PEAS**
1 tbsp **OLIVE OIL**
1 large **ONION**, *peeled, roughly chopped*
2 large **CARROTS**, *roughly chopped*
3 stalks **CELERY**, *roughly chopped*
2¼ ltrs (9 cups) **CHICKEN STOCK**
2 **BAY LEAVES AND PARSLEY STALKS**, *tied together*
1 **SMOKED BACON HOCK** *(approx 500g)*
1 cup **FRESH CURLY PARSLEY**, *roughly chopped*
SALT *and freshly* **GROUND BLACK PEPPER**

Place the split peas into a large bowl and cover with water. Discard any peas that float to the surface. Drain the remaining peas and rinse in a sieve with cold running water.

Heat the oil in a large saucepan over medium heat and cook the onion, carrot and celery for 10 minutes. Add the split peas, stock, bay leaves and parsley stalks and stir. Bring to the boil and add the hock. Reduce the heat to a simmer and cook for 1 hour or until the split peas are tender.

Remove the hock from the soup and shred the meat off it. Set this aside in a bowl and discard the skin and bone. Remove the parsley stalks and bay leaves from the soup and discard.

Blend the soup in the saucepan with a stick blender, or if you prefer leave it chunky. Add one or two cups of hot water if too thick after blending. Stir through the shredded meat and chopped parsley.

Season to taste with salt and freshly ground black pepper.

SMOKED FISH PIE

This has been one of our best sellers at Ripe. It freezes well and you can replace the gurnard with whatever white fish you like, or whatever you've been lucky enough to catch that day!

Serves 6-8

THE TOPPING

*1kg **POTATOES**, peeled and chopped into large pieces*

*⅓ cup (90ml) **CREAM***

*50g first measure of **BUTTER***

SALT** and freshly **GROUND BLACK PEPPER

*4 **EGGS***

*25g second measure of **BUTTER** for final assembly*

THE FISH

*400g **SMOKED FISH**, skin and any bones removed*

*400g **FRESH GURNARD FILLET**, skin and any bones removed*

*2½ cups (625ml) **MILK***

*1 cup (250ml) **CREAM***

*2 whole **ONIONS**, peeled, cut into rings*

*2 **BAY LEAVES***

THE WHITE SAUCE

*50g **BUTTER***

*⅓ cup (50g) plain **FLOUR***

*150g peeled cooked or raw **PRAWNS**, optional*

*¼ cup **FRESH CURLY PARSLEY**, roughly chopped*

*2 tbsp **FRESH DILL**, roughly chopped*

*2 tbsp **CAPERS**, rinsed*

ZEST** of 1 **LEMON

To prepare the topping: put your potatoes in a large saucepan. Cover with water and bring to the boil. Cook for approximately 20 minutes until soft. Strain the potatoes and place back in the saucepan with the cream, first measure of butter, salt and freshly ground black pepper. Mash well and set aside.

Hard boil your eggs, peel and roughly chop. Set aside.

Preheat oven to 200°C.

To cook the fish: put both types in a large saucepan. Pour over the milk and cream. Add the onion rings and bay leaves. Place over a medium heat and gently simmer for approximately 5 minutes or until just cooked. Remove from the heat and allow to cool.

Once cool, strain off the liquid into a bowl and set aside for the sauce. Reserve the fish and cooked onion. Discard the bay leaves.

To prepare the white sauce: place a large saucepan over a medium heat. Add the butter. When butter is melted add the flour to create a roux. Stir over a low heat for 1 minute (be careful not to burn). Gradually add the reserved liquid and beat constantly. Use a whisk to separate any lumps that form. Fold the reserved fish, cooked onion, eggs, prawns, parsley, dill, capers and zest into the sauce.

Season to taste with salt and pepper. Pour into a deep sided pie dish.

Cover with the mash. Using a fork, lightly fluff the top and dot with the second measure of butter for a crunchy finish. Bake in the oven for 30-40 minutes until heated through and golden on the top.

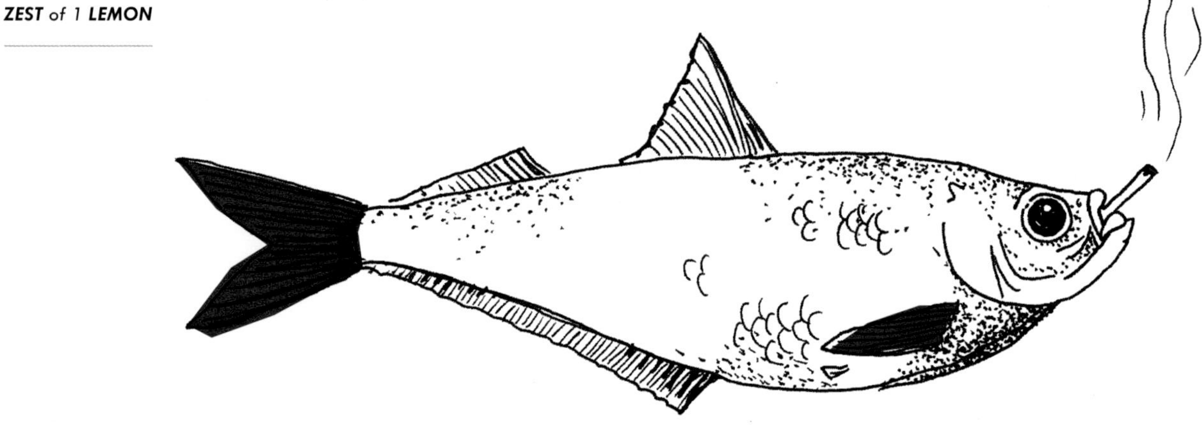

WHOLEMEAL LEEK & GOATS' CHEESE TART

Leeks are so good at this time of year. This tart makes a great lunch with a simple salad from The Greenhouse (see pg 64).

Serves 6-8

WHOLEMEAL PASTRY

1 cup (150g) ***WHOLEMEAL FLOUR***

½ cup (75g) plain ***FLOUR***

¼ tsp ***SALT***

125g ***UNSALTED BUTTER****, chilled and diced*

1 ***COURGETTE****, grated*

3-4 tbsp cold ***WATER***

FILLING

1 tbsp ***BUTTER***

3 tbsp ***OLIVE OIL***

1½ ***LEEKS****, split in half, cleaned and roughly chopped*

2 ***COURGETTES****, grated*

190g ***SOFT GOATS' CHEESE***

½ cup (125ml) ***CREAM***

4 ***EGGS***

SALT *and freshly* ***GROUND BLACK PEPPER***

To prepare the pastry: sift salt and the two flours into a mixing bowl, then add the butter and courgette.

Use your fingertips to quickly rub in the cold butter until the mixture resembles coarse bread crumbs. The colder your hands are for this step, the better. Sprinkle the water over the flour mixture and stir until the dough starts to hold together.

Bring the mixture together with your hands and knead very lightly to form a disc. Wrap with plastic wrap and chill in the fridge for 20 minutes.

Roll the pastry disc on a floured surface until it is large enough to cover the base and sides of a 20 x 25cm rectangle baking tin, or a 30cm round fluted tin.

Lay the pastry in the tin and press lightly into the edges and base, removing any overhanging pieces with a sharp knife. Prick holes in the base with a fork. Cover and re-chill in the fridge for 10 minutes.

Preheat oven to 200°C.

Blind bake (see pg 208) the chilled pastry for 15 minutes on the lowest shelf of your oven. Remove the baking weights and return to the oven for a further 5 minutes, then stand until ready for the filling.

To prepare the filling: place a large frying pan over a high heat. Melt the butter along with the olive oil. Add the leeks and cook for 5 minutes while stirring.

In a small bowl combine the courgettes, half of the goats' cheese, cream and eggs and whisk lightly. Season with salt and pepper. Add the cooked leeks and pour into the pastry base.

Crumble the other half of the goats' cheese over the tart and bake until the filling is set, approximately 15 minutes.

Delicious served either hot or cold.

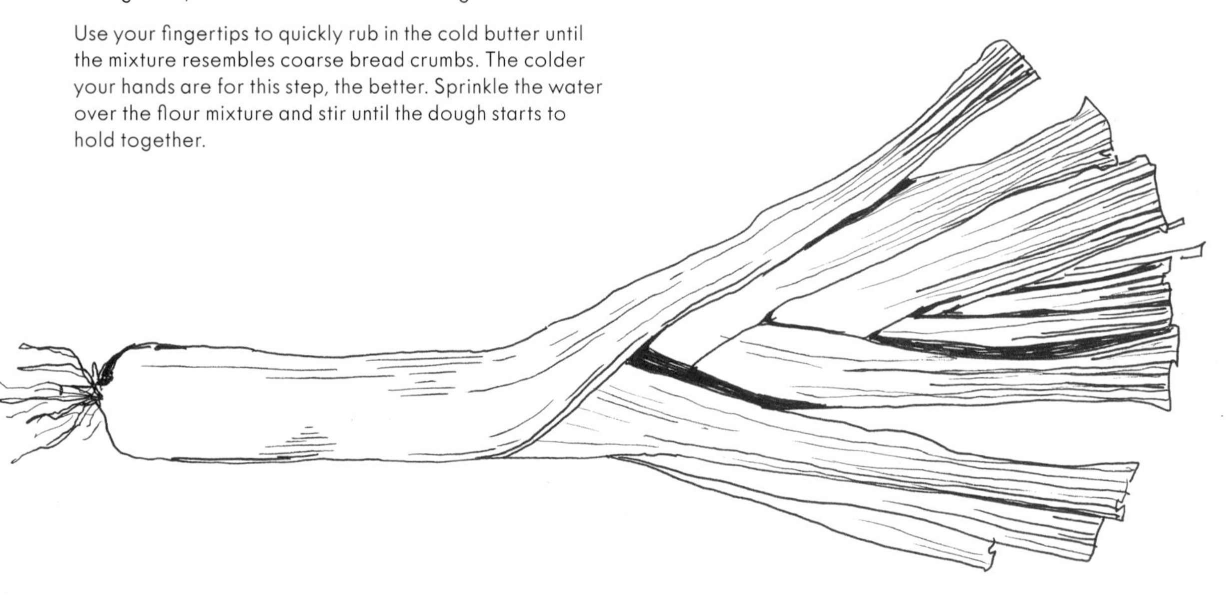

THAI CHICKEN NOODLE CAKES

Makes 6-8 large balls

700g ***CHICKEN MINCE***
300g ***DRIED EGG NOODLES***

THAI PASTE

1 tbsp ***FRESH GINGER****, peeled and roughly chopped*
1 tbsp ***FRESH GARLIC****, peeled and roughly chopped*
4 ***FRESH KAFFIR LIME LEAVES****, shredded*
1 cup ***FRESH CORIANDER LEAVES****, roughly chopped*
⅓ cup (80ml) ***FISH SAUCE***
1 cup (250ml) ***SWEET CHILLI SAUCE***
1 large handful of ***FRESH CORIANDER LEAVES*** *and* ***FRESH MINT LEAVES*** *to garnish*

Preheat oven to 180°C.

In a medium saucepan, cook the noodles in boiling water for 5 minutes then drain. Rinse under cold water and leave to cool.

To prepare the Thai paste: in a bowl or a food processor, combine the ginger, garlic, lime leaves, coriander, fish sauce and sweet chilli sauce, blending until you have a wet paste.

To prepare the noodle cakes: place the Thai paste in a large bowl with the chicken mince. Combine well. Add the noodles. Use your hands to squeeze the mixture together until the mince is evenly distributed.

Cover and chill for at least 30 minutes.

Once the mixture has chilled, remove from the fridge and roll into balls slightly smaller than tennis balls.

Place the noodle balls on a greased oven tray and bake for 30 minutes. Increase the heat to 200°C and cook until golden, approximately 5 minutes. Keep a close eye on them, to watch for burning.

Serve drizzled with your favourite sweet chilli sauce and garnish with the fresh coriander leaves and mint leaves. These can be served hot or cold.

This mix freezes well. Freeze the balls in raw form, then defrost overnight in the fridge and follow our cooking instructions as usual.

PEAR, PECAN & BLUE CHEESE SALAD

The balsamic reduction is sweet, sour and sticky. This quantity makes extra so keep some in a jar for another day.

Serves 4-6

SALAD

5 firm ***PEARS****, cored and sliced into thin strips, lengthways*
SALT *and freshly* ***GROUND BLACK PEPPER***
1 tbsp soft ***BROWN SUGAR***
1 tbsp ***OLIVE OIL***
4 large handfuls of ***FRESH ROCKET LEAVES***
1 cup (150g) ***PECAN NUTS*** *or* ***WALNUTS****, toasted and roughly chopped*
(see pg 211)
100g of your favourite ***SOFT BLUE CHEESE***
JUICE *of 1* ***LEMON***

BALSAMIC REDUCTION

1¼ cups (310ml) ***BALSAMIC VINEGAR***
1 cup (220g) ***WHITE SUGAR***

Preheat oven to 180°C.

Line a tray with baking paper and spread the sliced pears out on it. Sprinkle with a little salt, brown sugar and a drizzle of oil. Roast for 30 minutes. Remove and allow to cool.

To assemble the salad: on a large serving platter layer all the ingredients. Begin with the fresh rocket and follow with the pear, nuts, crumbled blue cheese and a healthy drizzle of the balsamic reduction. Repeat the layers and squeeze over the lemon juice to serve.

To prepare the balsamic reduction: combine the vinegar and sugar in a saucepan over a high heat. Bring to the boil then reduce heat and simmer for 10-15 minutes or until a thick syrup has formed. Keep an eye on it as it can overflow.

Season to taste with salt and pepper.

SMOKY CHORIZO AND ISRAELI COUSCOUS SALAD

Serves 4-6

1¼ cups (250g) ***ISRAELI COUSCOUS***
2 ***RED CAPSICUMS***
2 ***RED ONIONS****, peeled, cut into chunky wedges, layers separated*
1 tbsp ***SWEET CHILLI SAUCE***
3 cloves ***GARLIC****, peeled, cut into thin slivers*
3 ***CHORIZO SAUSAGES****, sliced into angled 1cm thick pieces*
½ cup (80g) ***KALAMATA OLIVES***
OLIVE OIL
2 tsp ***SMOKED PAPRIKA***
SALT *and freshly* ***GROUND BLACK PEPPER***
½ cup (80g) of your favourite ***GREEN STUFFED OLIVES***
4 ***TOMATOES****, cut into wedges*
1 cup ***FRESH ITALIAN PARSLEY****, roughly chopped*
1 cup ***FRESH CORIANDER LEAVES****, roughly chopped*
1 large handful of ***FRESH BABY SPINACH LEAVES***
1 cup ***SMOKED PAPRIKA DRESSING*** *(see pg 202)*

Preheat oven to 180°C.

Cook the couscous (see pg 210).

Core and de-seed the capsicums and cut into bite sized pieces, placing in a large bowl. Add the onion wedges, sweet chilli sauce, garlic, chorizo, kalamata olives and a good splash of oil. Sprinkle over the smoked paprika, a little salt and pepper and toss well to combine. Pour this into a deep sided oven roasting tray and roast for 30 minutes or until the chorizo and onions are starting to colour. Remove from the oven and allow to cool.

In a large serving bowl combine the roasted vegetable and chorizo mixture, cooked Israeli couscous, green olives, fresh tomato wedges, fresh herbs and spinach.

Drizzle over the smoked paprika dressing and mix gently. Season to taste with salt and freshly ground black pepper.

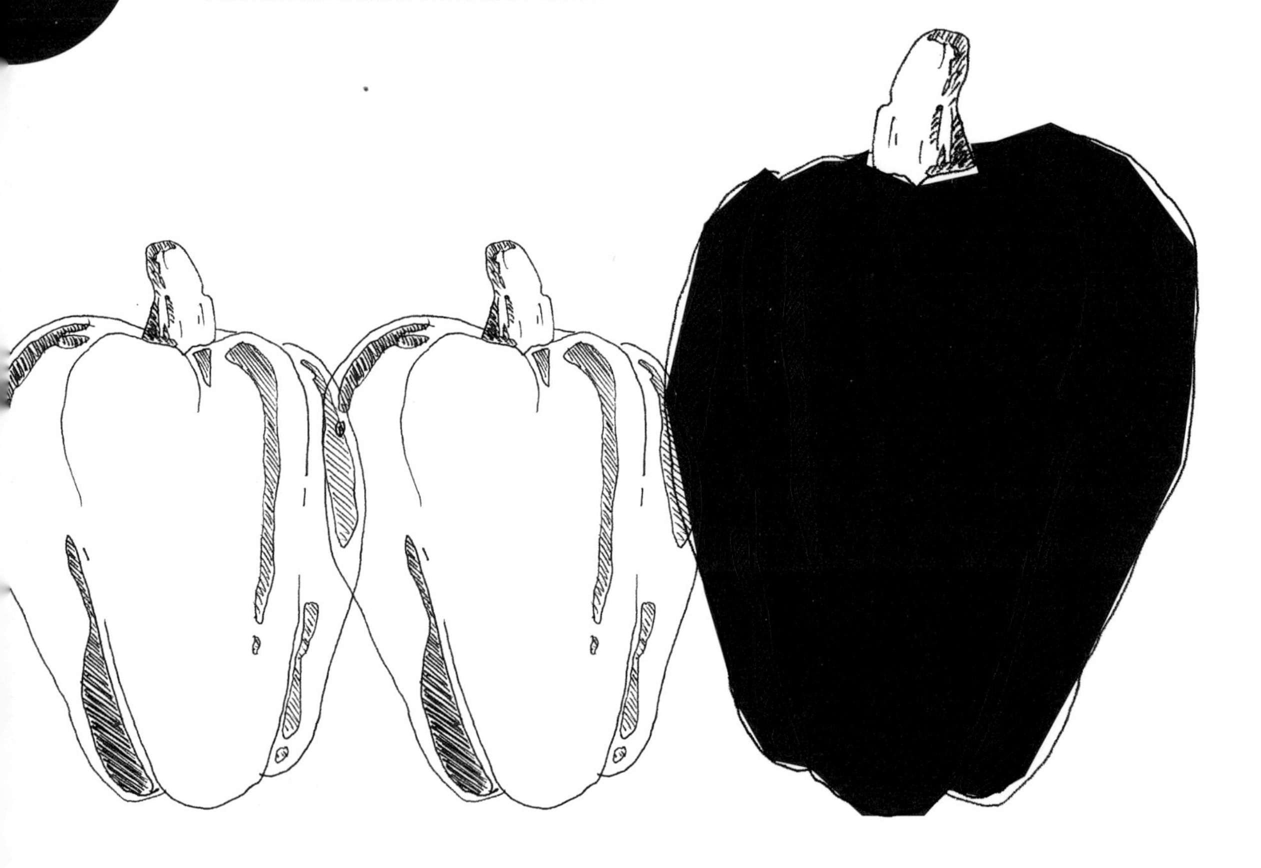

TUNA & CANNELLINI BEAN SALAD

Serves 4-6

1 cup (200g) ***CANNELLINI BEANS****, soaked overnight*
2 ***FENNEL BULBS****, roots trimmed*
1 tbsp soft ***BROWN SUGAR*** *or liquid honey*
JUICE *of 2* ***LEMONS***
4 large ***EGGS***
200g ***GREEN BEANS****, ends trimmed*
½ ***RED ONION****, sliced*
1 cup ***FRESH ITALIAN PARSLEY****, roughly chopped*
½ punnet ***CHERRY TOMATOES****, halved*
220g ***CANNED TUNA*** *in spring water*

DRESSING

½ cup (125ml) ***OLIVE OIL***
2 large handfuls of ***FRESH ROCKET LEAVES***
½ cup (40g) ***PARMESAN****, grated*
2 cloves ***GARLIC****, peeled and crushed*
SALT *and freshly* ***GROUND BLACK PEPPER***

Cook the cannellini beans (see pg 210).

Thinly slice the fennel and place in a bowl with the brown sugar and the lemon juice. Allow to marinate for 20 minutes.

Bring a small saucepan of water to the boil. Add the eggs and cook for 4 minutes. Allow to cool under cold running water, then peel and chop into quarters.

Bring another saucepan of water to the boil over a high heat and blanch the green beans for 2 minutes. Remove and refresh in iced water. Drain well.

To prepare the dressing: combine the olive oil, rocket, Parmesan and garlic in a bowl. Blend with a stick blender until thick and creamy. Taste and season with salt and pepper.

In a large serving bowl combine the cannellini and green beans, fennel, red onion, parsley, tomatoes and tuna. Pour over half of the dressing and toss together to incorporate the flavours. Dot the halved eggs around the bowl.

Taste and season with salt and pepper. Serve with the remainder of the dressing on the side.

PUMPKIN, SPINACH & OLIVE COUSCOUS SALAD

A delightful salad which complements our slow cooked lamb shanks (see pg 123) or baked green olive chicken (see pg 59). Makes a healthy lunch box salad served with a good dollop of cottage cheese and chopped chives.

Serves 4-6

⅓ cup (70g) **COUSCOUS**
⅓ cup (70g) **CHICKPEAS**, soaked overnight
¼ small (400g) **PUMPKIN**, peeled and diced finely
SALT and freshly **GROUND BLACK PEPPER**
OLIVE OIL
2 **RED CAPSICUMS**, roughly chopped
2 **COURGETTES**, cut into 1cm rounds
2 cloves **GARLIC**, peeled and crushed
½ cup (80g) **KALAMATA OLIVES**
1 handful of **FRESH SPINACH LEAVES**, roughly cut into shreds
½ cup (75g) **WHOLE ALMONDS**, roasted in oven
½ cup **FRESH MINT LEAVES**, roughly chopped, reserving some whole leaves for garnish
½ cup **FRESH ITALIAN PARSLEY**, roughly chopped
ZEST of 1 **LEMON**
1 cup **MINT DRESSING** (see pg 203)
½ cup (65g) **SUNFLOWER SEEDS**, toasted (see pg 211)
½ cup (65g) **PUMPKIN SEEDS**, toasted

Preheat oven to 180°C.

Soak the couscous. Cook the chickpeas (see pg 210).

Place the pumpkin on an oven roasting tray. Season well with salt and pepper and toss with enough olive oil to coat.

On another roasting tray place the capsicums, courgettes, garlic and olives. Season well with salt and pepper. Drizzle with enough olive oil to coat.

Bake both trays of vegetables for approximately 30 minutes or until tender and starting to brown.

Remove both trays from the oven and allow to cool.

To assemble the salad: combine in a large serving bowl all the cooked vegetables, cooked couscous, chickpeas, shredded spinach, almonds, fresh herbs and lemon zest. Drizzle over the mint dressing and mix gently to incorporate all the flavours.

Garnish with the fresh mint leaves and toasted seeds and serve.

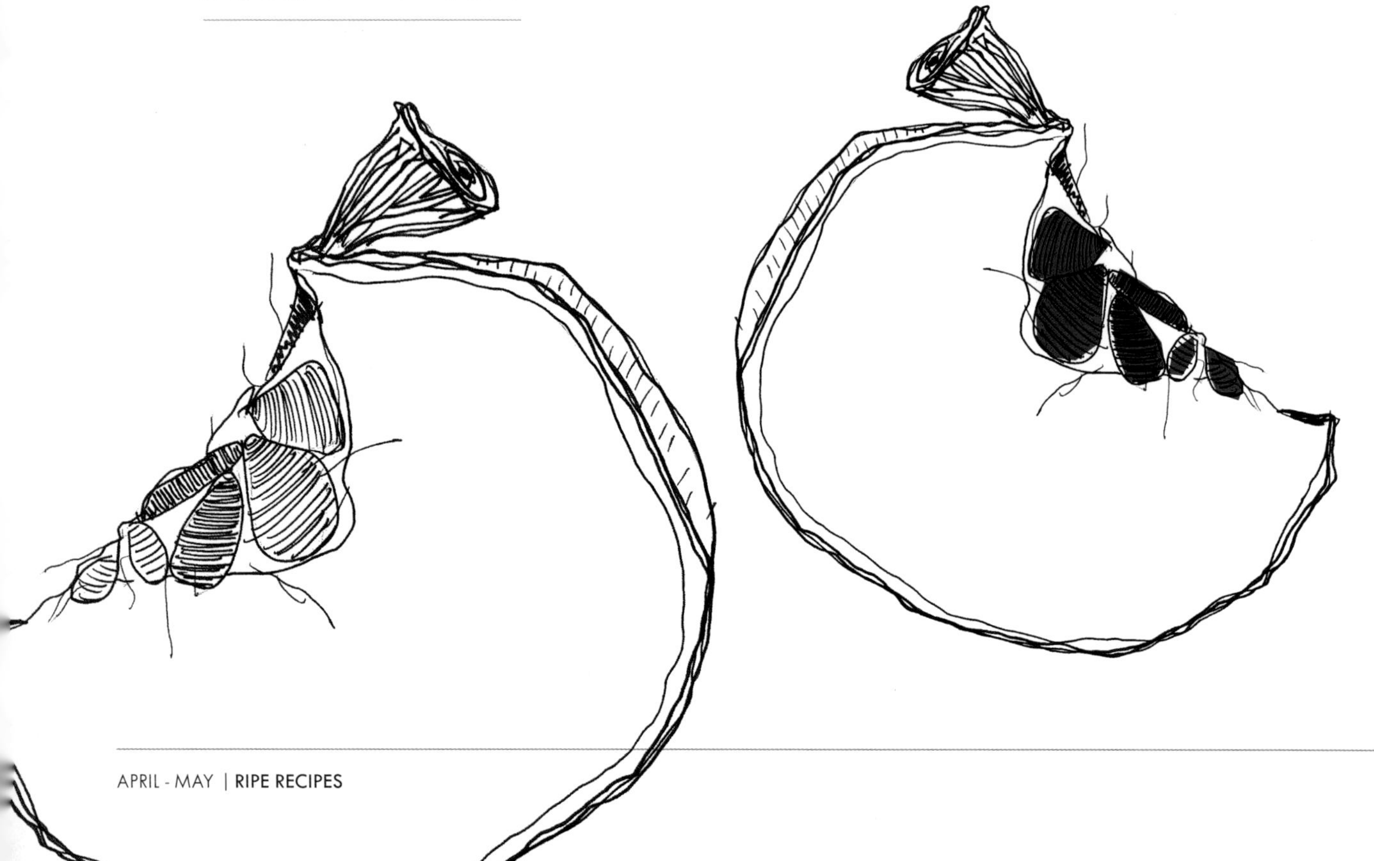

MAGIC SLICE

Ripe would love to take credit for inventing this one, but we found it on the back of a NESTLÉ condensed milk tin. Thank you very much NESTLÉ New Zealand.

*1½ (180g) cups **PLAIN SWEET BISCUITS**, crushed to a fine crumb*
*75g unsalted **BUTTER**, melted*
*1 cup **NESTLÉ** Milk or Dark **CHOC BITS***
*1 cup (160g) **RAISINS***
*1 cup (120g) **DESICCATED COCONUT***
*1 cup (120g) **SLICED ALMONDS***
*395g can **HIGHLANDER SWEETENED CONDENSED MILK***

Preheat oven to 180°C.

Grease and line a 20 x 30cm slice tin with baking paper.

Mix together the biscuit crumbs and melted butter. Press into the prepared slice tin with the back of a metal spoon. Cover and refrigerate to set for approximately 15 minutes.

In a large bowl place the NESTLÉ Milk CHOC BITS, raisins, coconut and almonds. Mix to combine. Pour over the HIGHLANDER Sweetened Condensed Milk and mix well until all the ingredients are coated and sticky.

Gently press the mixture evenly onto the top of the biscuit base.

Bake in the oven for 25-30 minutes until golden brown and firm to the touch.

Refrigerate well before cutting.

ROCKY RICHMOND ROAD SLICE

*250g **MALT BISCUITS**, crushed*
*250g **SUPER WINE BISCUITS**, crushed*
*250g **MARSHMALLOWS**, roughly chopped (mini marshmallows work just as well)*
*200g **UNSALTED BUTTER**, softened*
*1 cup (220g) **CASTER SUGAR***
*3 tbsp **COCOA**, sifted*
*3 large **EGGS**, lightly beaten*

ICING

*2 tbsp **COCOA**, sifted*
*1½ cups (190g) **ICING SUGAR**, sifted*
*50g **UNSALTED BUTTER**, melted*
*2 tbsp **LEMON JUICE***
*¼ cup (30g) **DESICCATED COCONUT***

Grease and line a 20 x 30cm slice tin.

Using a rolling pin, crush the biscuits in a double lined plastic bag to achieve a rough crumb.

Combine the biscuit crumbs and marshmallows in a bowl.

In a saucepan combine the butter, caster sugar and cocoa, stirring over a low heat until smooth. Add the lightly beaten eggs and cook for 5 minutes, stirring constantly. Remove from the heat and allow cool for 10 minutes.

Pour the mixture over the biscuit crumbs and marshmallows, mixing well. Press lightly into the prepared slice tin. Cover and cool in the fridge.

To prepare the icing: sift the icing sugar and cocoa together into a bowl. Add the melted butter, lemon juice and mix together. If the icing is a little stiff add hot water drop by drop to achieve a spreadable consistency. Spread on top of the cooled slice with a spatula and sprinkle with coconut.

St Pauls
school
ripe
Ponsonby
road
richmond rd
12
richmond rd
school
a. Lynn

RHUBARB BUTTERSCOTCH LAYER CAKE

Everyone needs an impressive layer cake recipe up their sleeve this may be the one! Our head baker – Lynn Colbert – wows us with this cake every time. It's been a real honour working alongside Lynn over the years.

When making the caramel for the icing, the boiling sugar must reach a dark colour to get a rich caramel flavour. A pale coloured caramel will lack intensity.

Serves 8-10

*225g **UNSALTED BUTTER**, softened*
*1 cup (160g) soft **BROWN SUGAR***
*100g **CASTER SUGAR***
*4 large **EGGS***
*1½ cups (225g) **SELF RAISING FLOUR***
*2-4 tbsp **CREAM***
*1 cup (150g) **RHUBARB**, chopped into 1cm pieces*

RHUBARB FILLING

*1½ cups (225g) **RHUBARB**, chopped into 1cm pieces*
*2 tbsp **CASTER SUGAR***

CARAMEL ICING

*300g **CASTER SUGAR***
*½ cup (125ml) cold **WATER***
*1 cup (250ml) **CREAM***
*400g **CREAM CHEESE**, softened*

Preheat oven to 180°C.

Grease two 21cm cake tins and line with baking paper.

In a food processor, blend together the butter, brown sugar, caster sugar, eggs and flour until smooth. Add the cream to achieve a runny, smooth consistency. Fold in rhubarb.

Divide and pour half into each tin. Bake for 25 minutes, or until a skewer inserted in the centre comes out clean.

The cakes may look small at this point, but they will look big and gorgeous when they are filled!

Cool cakes in their tins. Remove once they have cooled. Set aside.

To prepare the filling: place the rhubarb on a lined baking tray. Sprinkle with sugar and bake for 15 minutes until soft.

To prepare the caramel for the icing: place a medium sized saucepan over a medium heat. Add the sugar and water and keep stirring until the sugar is dissolved. At this stage stop stirring and bring the mixture to a boil.

Do not stir at all once boiling, or the sugar will crystallise. Don't leave the caramel unattended.

Continue boiling at a high heat for 10-15 minutes until the sugar reaches a hard boil and has turned a dark golden caramel colour. Remove from heat. With a whisk, start adding the cream gradually. Be careful as it can spit and foam up.

It can also form a lump, don't worry, just keep stirring. When all the cream has been added return to a low heat. Continue stirring for a minute until the caramel is smooth. Set aside to cool.

To prepare the icing: in a mixing bowl beat the cream cheese until smooth. Add 1 cup of the cold caramel. Mix well.

To assemble: lay the cooled cakes on a board and cut horizontally through the centre to make four even sized layers.

Divide the icing into four parts, one part to each layer of cake.

Place one layer of cake on a plate and with a spatula spread one quarter of the icing on. Don't worry about being too neat with the icing; a rustic approach results in a gorgeous cake. Then scatter on a quarter of the cooked rhubarb. Continue layering with the remaining sponges, rhubarb and icing.

Finally, drizzle over the remaining caramel for the perfect finish.

FEIJOA UPSIDE-DOWN CAKE

Gemma Heffernan is a great asset at Ripe. She's amazing on the customer floor and an even better baker. We thank Gemma for this recipe. This cake is equally delicious using pears or with the traditional tinned pineapple and cherries to garnish.

Serves 8-10

TOPPING

*50g **UNSALTED BUTTER***
*½ cup (80g) soft **BROWN SUGAR***
*6 large **FEIJOAS**, peeled and thinly sliced and tossed in*
***JUICE** of ½ **LEMON** to prevent browning*

CAKE

*50g **UNSALTED BUTTER**, softened*
*½ cup (110g) **CASTER SUGAR***
*1 **EGG***
*2 tsp **LEMON JUICE***
*½ cup (175g) **GOLDEN SYRUP***
*1½ cup (225g) plain **FLOUR***
*1 tsp **GROUND GINGER***
*1 tsp **GROUND CINNAMON***
*1 tsp **BAKING SODA***
*½ cup (125ml) **MILK***

Preheat oven to 170°C.

Grease and line a 24cm spring form cake tin with baking paper.

To prepare the topping: in a small saucepan over a low heat, melt together the butter and the brown sugar. Stir until the sugar has dissolved. Pour into the base of the prepared tin.

Arrange the feijoa pieces in an overlapping circular pattern on top of the melted butter and sugar. Set aside. Careful placement of your fruit is a must, as this is where the finished beauty lies.

To prepare the cake: in a large bowl or electric mixer cream together the softened butter and caster sugar until light and fluffy. Add the egg, lemon juice and golden syrup and mix to combine.

In a separate bowl, sift together the flour, ginger and cinnamon. In another small bowl, dissolve the baking soda in the milk. Alternating between the milk and dry ingredients, add to the creamed butter, starting and finishing with the dry. Mix until combined, then pour the cake batter carefully over the feijoas in the tin.

Bake the cake for 30-40 minutes or until springy to the touch. Remove the cake from the oven and allow to cool.

Before turning the cake out onto a serving plate run a knife around the edge to release. Place a large serving plate over the top of the cake. Gripping the tin and plate together, flip over and place the cake plate side down. Carefully release the spring form tin and remove the baking paper.

Serve with whipped cinnamon cream (see pg 208) or custard.

QUINCE & APPLE TARTE TATIN

We really wanted to find a good way to use quinces, as so many of our customers have brought them to our Market Garden. Quince paste and jelly are delicious, and so is this classic French tarte tatin. Quinces can be quite sour, which is why it's best to use apples in the recipe as well.

Serve with crème fraiche. We recommend Gala, Braeburn or Golden Delicious apples.

Serves 4-6

1-2 sheets (500g) ***BUTTER PUFF PASTRY***
100g ***UNSALTED BUTTER***
150g ***CASTER SUGAR***
3-4 medium sized ***APPLES****, peeled, cored and cut into eighths*
1 ***QUINCE****, peeled, cored and cut into twelve pieces (thinner than the apple)*
GROUND CINNAMON *to dust the tart before serving (optional)*

Preheat oven to 200°C.

Cut the pastry into a circle slightly larger than a 26cm ovenproof frying pan or a shallow sponge cake tin.

In the ovenproof frying pan, melt the butter over a medium heat. Once the butter starts to foam add the sugar. Stir to dissolve and remove from the heat. Add the apple and quince and arrange in a tight fitting circular pattern. Begin in the centre of the pan and radiate outwards.

Place the fruit back on the heat – increase to high. Cook until the butter, sugar and fruit juices begin to caramelise and the fruit begins to soften, approximately 10 minutes. Keep an eye on it and reduce the heat if necessary. Remove from heat when all golden.

NOTE: If you do not have an ovenproof frying pan, cook the caramel and fruit as mentioned in a normal frying pan and then tip the caramel and fruit into a shallow sponge cake tin. Rearrange the fruit on top and carry on with the recipe. Be careful. It will be hot!

Lay the pastry on top of the fruit and tuck the pastry down around the inner edge of the pan (this is so it traps the caramel when you flip it over after cooking. It acts like a saucer). Bake in the hot oven for 20-30 minutes, or until the pastry is golden brown and caramel is bubbling at the edges.

Remove from the oven and allow to cool for 5-10 minutes. Using a blunt knife, run around the edge of the pastry to release it.

Place a plate larger than the circumference of the pan or tin over the tarte. Carefully flip over the pan so that the fruit is on the top and the pastry on the bottom. Take care when lifting the pan, as steam and caramel may escape.

Dust lightly with cinnamon and serve with ice cream or whipped cream.

GEORGE'S ROAST BANANA CHEESECAKE

Former head chef Louise Kelleher introduced this cheesecake to Ripe, which is now officially named after its biggest fan, George Henare. Louise's caring and infectious personality is missed at Ripe (not to mention her piping bag skills!).

Serves 8-10

BASE

250g ***MALT****, Gingernut or Digestive* ***BISCUITS***
100g ***BUTTER****, melted*

ROAST BANANA FILLING

4 ***BANANAS***
1kg ***CREAM CHEESE***
1 cup (220g) ***CASTER SUGAR***
6 ***EGGS***

TOPPING

1 ***BANANA***
1 tbsp ***BUTTER***
1 tbsp white ***SUGAR***
½ cup (175g) ***MAPLE SYRUP*** *to glaze*

Preheat oven to 170°C.

Grease and line a 26cm spring form tin with baking paper.

To prepare the base: place the biscuits and butter into a food processor and blend until they form a wet sandy consistency. Transfer mixture into the lined tin and press down with the back of a spoon. Cover and chill in the fridge.

To prepare the filling: put the unpeeled bananas on a lined baking tray and bake until black and soft, approximately 15 minutes. Set aside to cool.

In the cleaned food processor bowl place the cream cheese, sugar and eggs and process until smooth and well combined.

Split and peel the cooled bananas and add to cream cheese mixture. Process until well combined.

Pour onto the chilled biscuit base and bake for 45 minutes. At this point give the tin a gentle jiggle – if the surface stays set together on top it's ready to remove from the oven.

For best results chill in the fridge overnight.

To prepare the topping: peel and slice the banana in half lengthways. Melt the butter and sugar in a small frying pan. Add the banana and cook over a medium to high heat until slightly caramalised. Allow to cool.

Before releasing from the tin, pour over the maple syrup as a glaze and pile the banana on top.

George & Ginny enjoying a slice!

GET READY TO RUMBLE WITH CRUMBLE

Fruit crumble is fantastic for breakfast with yoghurt or as a dessert served with vanilla custard.

We have given you a few fruit and crumble options. Have fun mixing and matching, as they will all work well together. All recipes serve 6-8 people.

BASIC CRUMBLE RECIPE

*100g **UNSALTED BUTTER**, cut into 1cm cubes*
*1 cup (150g) plain **FLOUR** or wholemeal flour*
*1 cup (90g) **ROLLED OATS***
*½ cup (80g) soft **BROWN SUGAR***

CRUMBLE VARIATIONS

Add one or two of the following:
*½ cup (35g) **LONG THREAD COCONUT***
*50g **PECANS**, chopped*
*50g sliced **ALMONDS***
*½ cup of your favourite **MUESLI***
*1 tsp **GROUND CINNAMON** or ½ tsp ground nutmeg*
*1 tsp **GROUND GINGER** or 2 cubes crystallised ginger, sliced finely*

Preheat oven to 180°C.

In a large bowl rub the butter into the flour. Stir in the rolled oats and brown sugar.

Add a variation if you wish, avoiding dried fruit as it tends to burn.

Spoon the stewed fruit into your favourite deep sided ovenproof dish.

Top your stewed fruit with the crumble mixture. The crumble topping should be about 1cm deep. Keep a higher ratio of fruit to crumble. Bake for 20-30 minutes or until the crumble topping is golden in colour.

ROASTED RHUBARB & ORANGE

*1½ kg **RHUBARB** stalks*
*1 cup (160g) soft **BROWN SUGAR***
JUICE** and **ZEST** of 1 **ORANGE

Preheat oven to 180°C.

Wash and cut the rhubarb into 4cm long pieces. Place on a paper lined oven tray. Sprinkle with brown sugar. Pour over the zest and juice and lightly toss.

Bake for approximately 15 minutes. Remove and allow to cool. This method softens and sweetens the rhubarb beautifully, without it turning to mush.

POACHED TAMARILLO & APPLE

*½kg **TAMARILLOS**, approx*
*½ cup (125ml) **ORANGE JUICE***
*½ cup (80g) soft **BROWN SUGAR***
*1kg **APPLES***

Peel the tamarillos and slice thickly. Place into a bowl. Add the orange juice and sprinkle over the soft brown sugar. Peel and slice the apples. Mix with the tamarillos.

Place the tamarillo mixture into a saucepan over a medium heat and cook until the fruit is tender. Remove from the heat and allow to cool.

POACHED FEIJOA & APPLE

*½kg of fresh **FEIJOAS**, approx*
*1kg **APPLES***
*¼ cup (60ml) **LEMON JUICE***
*¼ cup (40g) soft **BROWN SUGAR***

Peel the feijoas and apples and slice thickly. Place into a bowl. Add the lemon juice and sprinkle over the soft brown sugar.

Place mixture into a saucepan over a medium heat and cook until the fruit is tender. Remove from heat and allow to cool.

FEIJOA & GINGER JAM

This jam has a gorgeous colour and an intense feijoa flavour. Swirl it through your muffin mix or add to your brioche dough.

Makes approximately 1.25 litres

750g freshly peeled ***FEIJOAS***
750g ***WHITE SUGAR***
3cm ***FRESH GINGER****, grated, or 2 tbsp preserved ginger, finely sliced*

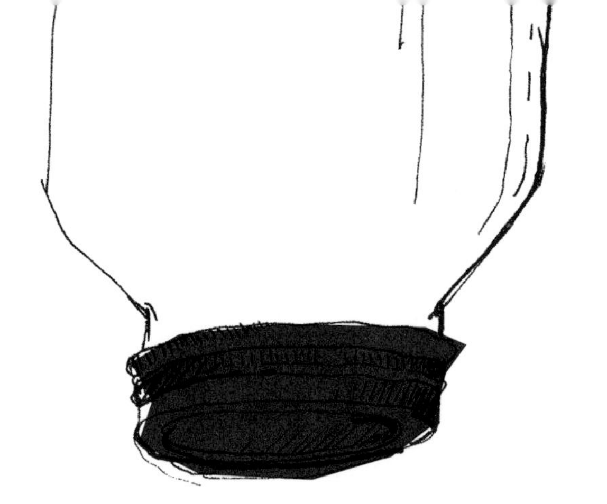

Roughly chop the feijoa flesh.

In a large saucepan over a medium heat, add the feijoa pulp. Gently stir until the fruit starts to soften and break down. This takes approximately 20 minutes. Add the sugar and ginger and gently boil for a further 20 minutes.

The jam is ready when the mixture has thickened a little. Drop a spoonful onto a saucer to check the setting point (see pg 209).

Pour the hot jam into sterilised jars and seal (see pg 209).

PEAR & DATE CHUTNEY

A recipe from my mother, Jane Redfern. This is quite a sweet chutney that I love with blue cheese and crackers.

Makes approximately 3 litres

12 ***PEARS****, skin on, small rough chop*
4 cups (1 ltr) ***MALT VINEGAR***
50g ***PRESERVED GINGER****, roughly chopped*
50g ***SALT***
4 cloves ***GARLIC****, finely chopped*
2½ cups (425g) soft ***BROWN SUGAR***
500g ***RAISINS***
500g ***DRIED DATES****, roughly chopped*
1 tsp ***CAYENNE PEPPER***

In a large saucepan over a medium heat, combine the pears and malt vinegar and cook until the pears have softened, approximately 20 minutes.

Add the remaining ingredients to the saucepan and bring to the boil. Once boiling, reduce the heat and continue to cook the chutney until it has thickened, approximately 40 minutes.

Pour the hot chutney into sterilised jars and seal (see pg 209).

Ideally, leave the chutney for a few days to allow the flavours to mature before use.

TAMARILLO CHUTNEY

Makes approximately 2 litres

12 ***TAMARILLOS***
¼ cup ***OLIVE OIL***
2 large ***ONIONS****, peeled, diced into 1cm pieces*
6 ***APPLES****, peeled and diced into 1cm cubes*
2 cups (500ml) ***APPLE CIDER VINEGAR***
2½ cups (425g) soft ***BROWN SUGAR***
1 tbsp ***SALT***
1 tsp ***MIXED SPICE***
1 tsp ***CAYENNE PEPPER***

Score the tamarillos on the end (mark an "X" with a sharp knife).

Bring a large saucepan of water to the boil over a high heat. Add the tamarillos to the boiling water and cook for 2 minutes. Remove and quickly plunge into a bowl of iced water. Once cooled, drain, peel and roughly chop. Set aside.

In a large saucepan over a medium heat, add the oil and cook the onion for 5 minutes or until soft. Add the tamarillos and apple and cook for a couple of minutes. Add the vinegar, sugar, salt, mixed spice and cayenne pepper. Simmer on a low heat for 1 hour, adding water if the chutney thickens too quickly.

Spoon the hot chutney into sterilised jars and seal. (see pg 209).

"Put a lid on it" – Anon

Jerusalem artichoke. Parsley. Cauliflower. Broccoli. Brussel sprouts. Lemons. Persimmons. Limes. Oranges. Grapefruits. Mandarins. Silverbeet. Spinach. Winter salad greens. Kumara.

JUNE | JULY

It's a pleasure walking into Ripe on a cold winter's morning. There is a buzz in the air created by the wonderful people in the store. The smell of morning baking and hot coffee makes for a good start to any day!

SENORITA'S EGG, SAUSAGE & BEANS

This makes a delicious quick Sunday brunch, especially if you have a few mouths to feed. It looks great served in a paella pan. A big thank you to Kylie Wilson for this tasty recipe. Kylie has been a loyal and close colleague at Ripe for many years.

Serves 6-8

3 tbsp **OLIVE OIL**
2 small **RED ONIONS**, peeled, finely diced
3 cloves **GARLIC**, peeled and crushed
250g **CHORIZO SAUSAGES**, roughly chopped
2 tsp **SMOKED PAPRIKA**
3 x 400g can **TOMATOES**, chopped
1 tbsp **TOMATO PASTE**
1 tbsp **WORCESTERSHIRE SAUCE**
2 tbsp soft **BROWN SUGAR**
1 tbsp **RED WINE VINEGAR**
2 x 400g canned **CANNELLINI BEANS**, drained
1 cup **FRESH ITALIAN PARSLEY**, roughly chopped
1 tsp **SALT**
1 tsp freshly **GROUND BLACK PEPPER**
8 **EGGS**
¼ cup (20g) **PARMESAN**, finely grated

Preheat oven to 180°C.

Place a large frying pan on a medium heat. Add the olive oil and cook the onions and garlic for 5 to 10 minutes or until soft. Add the chorizo and sprinkle over the smoked paprika.

Cook for a few minutes until the chorizo is lightly browned. Add the chopped tomatoes, tomato paste, Worcestershire sauce, sugar and red wine vinegar.

Bring to the boil. Lower the heat and simmer uncovered for 20 minutes. At this point add the cannellini beans and ¾ of the chopped parsley. Season with salt and pepper.

Pour the hot mixture into a large ovenproof dish or paella pan if you have one. Spread out evenly and crack the eggs on top.

Bake uncovered for 15-20 minutes or until the eggs are cooked to your liking.

Remove from oven and sprinkle with Parmesan, the remaining parsley and a pinch of smoked paprika.

Serve with lots of hot fresh bread or toast.

ALTA MUFFIN

My friend, Alta (which translates to "ultimate"), was the inspiration for us to produce this healthy high fibre muffin. Lynn Colbert has done a great job of creating this muffin which has led to an improvement in all of our digestive systems here at Ripe. This recipe contains linseed which is a great source of our good friend fibre.

LSA is a mix of ground linseed, sunflower seeds and almonds, readily available in supermarkets.

Makes approximately 12 muffins

1 cup (250ml) ***VEGETABLE OIL*** *or sunflower oil*
1 cup (160g) soft ***BROWN SUGAR***
4 ***EGGS***
2 ripe ***BANANAS****, mashed roughly*
1 cup ***TINNED PEACHES*** *or plums, drained and roughly chopped*
ZEST *of 2* ***ORANGES***
1 cup ***BLUEBERRIES****, frozen*
½ cup (55g) ***LSA***
1½ cups (90g) ***BAKING BRAN***
2 cups (300g) ***SPELT FLOUR***
2 tsp ***GROUND CINNAMON***
3 tsp ***BAKING SODA***

Preheat oven to 180°C.

Use two standard muffin trays and line with paper muffin cases or grease well.

In a large bowl whisk the oil, brown sugar and eggs.

Fold the mashed bananas, peaches, orange zest and blueberries in gently.

In another bowl mix the LSA, baking bran, spelt flour, cinnamon and baking soda.

Fold the dry ingredients into the wet mixture until just combined. It's very important not to overmix or you will have chewy, tough muffins.

Note: at this stage you can refrigerate some of the mixture to use the next day.

Spoon the mixture into the muffin cases and bake for 30-35 minutes or until a skewer pushed into the centre comes out clean.

SWEET SWEET MUFFINS

"Ahhh, what flavour are the sweet sweet muffins today?" asks Leigh. "Apple, pecan, and maple," we reply. "Ahhh, that's my favourite!" says Leigh. It's the same response every day for every flavour we make.

Just one of the daily rituals we look forward to from one of our favourite customers!

Makes 12

200g ***UNSALTED BUTTER***
4 large ***EGGS***
1 cup (250ml) ***MILK***
½ tsp ***VANILLA EXTRACT***
1 cup (220g) ***CASTER SUGAR***
2 cups ***FRUIT*** *(see below for suggestions)*
4 cups (600g) ***SELF RAISING FLOUR***
2 tsp ***GROUND CINNAMON***

Preheat oven to 180°C.

Grease muffin tins or line with paper cases.

Melt the butter and leave to cool a little.

In a large bowl, combine together the eggs, milk, vanilla and sugar.

Add your favourite flavour combination (opposite) to the wet mix.

Add flour, cinnamon and melted butter. Gently fold together until combined. Don't overmix. Spoon into the muffin cups until ⅔ full. Bake for 20 minutes until firm to the touch.

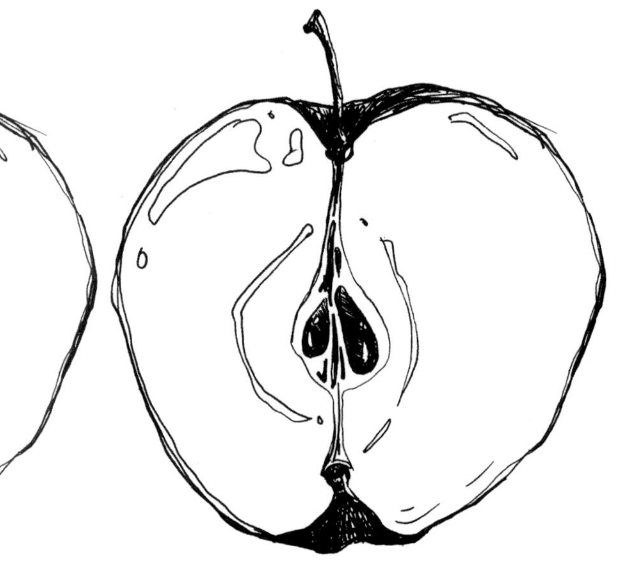

APPLE & PECAN

1 cup chopped apple and 1 cup chopped pecans, with a drizzle of maple syrup on top once out of oven.

FEIJOA & PEAR

1 cup feijoa pulp and 1 cup chopped fresh pears.

BLUEBERRY & ORANGE

1 cup frozen berries and zest of 2 oranges.

WHITE CHOCOLATE & RASPBERRIES

1 cup white chocolate chips and 1 cup frozen berries.

PEAR & PRESERVED GINGER

1 cup chopped pear and ¼ cup sliced preserved ginger.

RHUBARB & APPLE

1 cup chopped rhubarb and 1 cup chopped apple.

PASSION FRUIT & COCONUT

1 cup long thread coconut and ½ cup passion fruit pulp.

PLUM & CREAM CHEESE

1 cup chopped pitted plums, fresh or tinned. Add ½ tsp of cream cheese to the centre of each muffin before baking.

SAVOURY CHEESE SCONES

Fabulous for breakfast or morning tea, these scones are also great with soup. Make them with or without the bacon.

Makes 6 large scones

2 cups (300g) plain ***FLOUR***
2 tsp ***BAKING POWDER***
1 tsp ***SALT***
1 tsp freshly ***GROUND BLACK PEPPER***
50g ***UNSALTED BUTTER****, cold*
½ cup ***FRESH CURLY PARSLEY****, finely chopped*
1 whole fresh ***TOMATO****, diced*
1 cup (120g) ***TASTY CHEESE****, grated*
100g diced cooked ***BACON*** *or ham (optional)*
½ cup (125ml) ***MILK****, approx*

Preheat oven to 200°C.

Grease an oven tray or line with baking paper.

In a large bowl, sift together the flour, baking powder, salt and pepper.

Dice up the cold butter and rub it into the dry mixture using your fingertips until it resembles coarse bread crumbs. Add the parsley, tomato, grated cheese and cooked bacon, combining well.

Add enough milk to lightly combine, stirring lightly. Be careful not to overmix as this will toughen the scones. On a lightly floured surface, empty the mixture from the bowl and pat it together.

Cut the dough into six pieces, shape carefully, and place them on the prepared baking tray. Brush with milk to glaze. Bake for 10-15 minutes, or until golden.

JERUSALEM ARTICHOKE SOUP

A thick hearty soup, made luxurious with the addition of creamy blue cheese.

Serves 4-6

50g ***BUTTER***
2 tbsp ***OLIVE OIL***
1 ***ONION****, peeled, roughly chopped*
6-8 cloves ***GARLIC****, peeled and sliced*
½ ***LEEK****, white part, roughly chopped*
2 stalks ***CELERY****, roughly chopped*
800g ***JERUSALEM ARTICHOKES****, scrubbed and roughly chopped*
½ ***CARROT****, peeled and roughly chopped*
SALT *and freshly* ***GROUND BLACK PEPPER***
1 ***BAY LEAF***
8 cups (2ltr) ***VEGETABLE STOCK***
6 cups (1½ltr) ***WATER***
½ cup (125ml) ***CREAM***
50g ***BLUE CHEESE****, crumbled*

Place a large saucepan over a medium heat. Melt the butter along with the oil. Add the onion, garlic, leek, celery and cook for 5 minutes. Add the artichokes and carrot and cook for a further 5 minutes.

Add half a teaspoon each of salt and pepper, bay leaf, then stock and water.

Increase the heat and bring to the boil. Lower the heat to a simmer. Cook for approximately 1 hour or until the vegetables have softened.

Purée with a stick blender or blend in a food processor until smooth. Add a little more water if soup is too thick. Add the cream and crumbled blue cheese and mix until combined.

Season to taste with salt and pepper. The taste of this soup can be intensified by crumbling over more blue cheese.

SLOW COOKED LAMB SHANKS

There are two different sized lamb shanks you can buy – large ones from the hindquarter and smaller ones from the forequarter. We recommend the larger ones as there is more tender meat on them when cooked.

Remember to allow a good 3 hours cooking time for this dish. It's a good idea to have your ingredients prepared before you start cooking. Leftovers will make a great pie filling or soup base. If you want to cook less than six shanks, adjust the ingredient quantities accordingly, otherwise your sauce will be lacking in flavour.

This freezes well too and is one of those dishes that will taste even better the next day. Serve with a mash from the S&M pages (see pg 160).

Serves 6

1 tbsp plain ***FLOUR***
1 tsp ***GROUND CORIANDER***
1½ tsp ***GROUND CUMIN***
1 tsp ***GROUND CINNAMON***
1 tsp ***DRIED OREGANO***
½ tsp ***DRIED CHILLI FLAKES***
½ tsp ***SALT***
¼ tsp freshly ***GROUND BLACK PEPPER***
6 hind quarter ***LAMB SHANKS***
VEGETABLE OIL *to rub on shanks*
6 tbsp ***OLIVE OIL***
1 ***ONION****, peeled, thinly sliced*
6 cloves ***GARLIC****, peeled, roughly chopped*
1 large ***CARROT****, roughly chopped*
1 ***LEEK****, white part only, roughly chopped*
2 stalks ***CELERY****, roughly chopped*
4 sprigs ***FRESH ROSEMARY****, leaves picked and finely chopped*
1 ***BAY LEAF****, crushed*
1 cup (250ml) ***WHITE WINE***
1½ cups (375ml) ***CHICKEN STOCK***
2 x 400g can ***CRUSHED TOMATOES***
400g can ***CANNELLINI BEANS****, strained and rinsed*
6-8 ***ANCHOVY FILLETS****, finely chopped*
JUICE *and* ***ZEST*** *of 1* ***LEMON***
½ cup ***FRESH ITALIAN PARSLEY****, finely chopped*

Preheat oven to 180°C.

In a large bowl, combine the flour, coriander, cumin, cinnamon, oregano, chilli, salt and pepper. Rub a little oil on the lamb shanks and roll in the seasoned flour, pressing as much as possible onto the meat.

In a large frying pan heat half of the olive oil until it reaches smoking point.

Brown the lamb shanks on all sides. You will need to do this in batches so as not to overcrowd the frying pan. Remove the shanks and place them in a large casserole dish and set aside.

Add the remaining oil to the frying pan and cook the onion, garlic, carrot, leek and celery for 5 minutes over a medium heat. Add the rosemary, bay leaf, wine, stock, tomatoes and any of the seasoned flour that was left over. Stir through and bring gently to the boil. Pour this over the lamb shanks in the casserole dish. Arrange the shanks so that they are mostly covered by the sauce.

Cover and cook in the oven for 2 hours, turning once.

After 2 hours, remove from the oven. Add the beans, mix through gently and continue cooking for another hour. By now the meat should be tender and falling from the shank.

Finally, in a small bowl place the finely chopped anchovies, lemon juice, zest and parsley and stir to blend.

Mix this through the casserole just before you serve adding some more freshly ground pepper to taste.

"Few peas short of a casserole." – Coronation Street

KUSHARI

This popular Egyptian national dish often – transliterated as koshary or kosheri – will soon become one of your new favourite comfort foods.

Serves 4-6

LENTILS AND RICE

1 cup (200g) **GREEN LENTILS**
50g **BUTTER**
1 cup (200g) **BASMATI RICE**
2 cups (500ml) **CHICKEN STOCK**
1 tsp **SUMAC**
1 tsp **FRESH NUTMEG**, *grated or ground nutmeg*
1½ tsp **GROUND CINNAMON**
1½ tsp **SALT**
½ tsp freshly **GROUND BLACK PEPPER**
¼ cup **OLIVE OIL**
2 **ONIONS**, *peeled and thinly sliced*
1 cup (150g) **PISTACHIOS**, *toasted (see pg 211)*
1 cup **FRESH ITALIAN PARSLEY**, *roughly chopped*
1 cup **FRESH CORIANDER LEAVES**, *roughly chopped*

SPICY TOMATO SAUCE

¼ cup **OLIVE OIL**
3 cloves **GARLIC**, *peeled and crushed*
3 **RED CHILLIES**, *seeds removed and finely sliced*
400g can **CRUSHED TOMATOES**
1½ cups (375ml) **WATER**
¼ cup **CIDER VINEGAR**
1 tsp **SALT**
1 tsp **GROUND CUMIN**
1 tsp **PAPRIKA**
¼ cup **FRESH CORIANDER LEAVES**, *finely chopped*

Cook the lentils (see pg 210).

To prepare the spicy tomato sauce: place a saucepan over a high heat. Add the oil, garlic and chillies and cook for 3 minutes.

Add the tomatoes, water, vinegar, salt, cumin and paprika. Bring to the boil and lower the heat. Simmer for 30 minutes or until thickened.

Stir in the fresh coriander leaves. Taste to see if more salt, pepper or coriander needs to be added.

To prepare the rice: place a saucepan over a high heat. Melt the butter and add the rice. Cook for 1 minute, stirring constantly. Add the stock or water, sumac, nutmeg, cinnamon, salt and pepper.

Bring to the boil, then reduce to a low simmer and cook for 12 minutes before removing from the heat. Cover and set aside for 12 minutes. While the rice is resting prepare the onions.

In a large frying pan, heat the olive oil to a medium heat and slowly cook the onions until dark gold in colour. This should take approximately 20 minutes.

Break the cooked rice up with a fork.

In a large bowl mix together the cooked lentils, rice, toasted pistachios, fresh parsley, coriander and ⅔ of the cooked onions.

Season with salt and pepper and pile high on a platter. Top with the remainder of the onions and serve with the spicy tomato sauce.

CHILLI SQUID WITH BUTTERNUT SALAD

Serves 4-6

SQUID AND MARINADE

6-8 ***SQUID TUBES***
1 tbsp ***SOY SAUCE***
3 tbsp ***OLIVE OIL***
2 tbsp ***WHITE WINE VINEGAR***
8 cloves ***GARLIC****, crushed*
2 tbsp ***FRESH GINGER****, peeled and chopped finely*
1 tbsp ***LEMON GRASS****, sliced finely*
JUICE *of 3* ***LEMONS***
JUICE *of 4* ***LIMES***
⅓ cup (80ml) ***FISH SAUCE***
3 tbsp soft ***BROWN SUGAR***
1 ***SPRING ONION****, finely chopped*
1 small ***RED ONION****, peeled, finely chopped*
2 ***BIRDSEYE CHILLIES****, de-seeded and finely chopped*

SALAD

1kg ***BUTTERNUT PUMPKIN***
2 tbsp ***PEANUT OIL***
Freshly ***GROUND BLACK PEPPER***
1 ***COS LETTUCE****, leaves finely shredded*
½ ***LEBANESE CUCUMBER****, thinly sliced*
1 cup ***FRESH CORIANDER LEAVES****, roughly chopped*
½ cup ***FRESH MINT LEAVES****, roughly chopped*
1 cup (165g) ***ROASTED UNSALTED PEANUTS****, roughly chopped*

Preheat oven to 200°C.

To prepare the squid: cut through one side so that they lay as a single sheet. Score the squid crossways on the inner side with a sharp knife.

Cut into strips between 1 and 1½cm wide. Place the squid strips into a small bowl, adding the soy sauce and tossing to coat.

In a wok or saucepan, add the oil and bring to smoking point. Cook the squid quickly in batches until tender, approximately 30 seconds.

Drain on paper towels and allow to cool.

To prepare the marinade: combine the vinegar, garlic, ginger, lemon grass, lemon and lime juices, fish sauce, brown sugar, spring onion, red onion and chilli in a bowl. Add the cooked squid and keep covered in the fridge for 1 hour to marinate.

Chop the butternut in half and scoop out the seeds. Peel and chop into 2cm cubes.

Place the cubes onto an oven roasting tray and drizzle with the peanut oil. Season with pepper and toss to coat. Roast in the oven for 30 minutes or until tender.

To assemble the salad: spread out the roasted butternut on a large platter. Combine the lettuce, cucumber, squid, fresh coriander leaves and mint. Layer the salad over the butternut, and drizzle with some of the remaining marinade. Sprinkle over the toasted peanuts and serve.

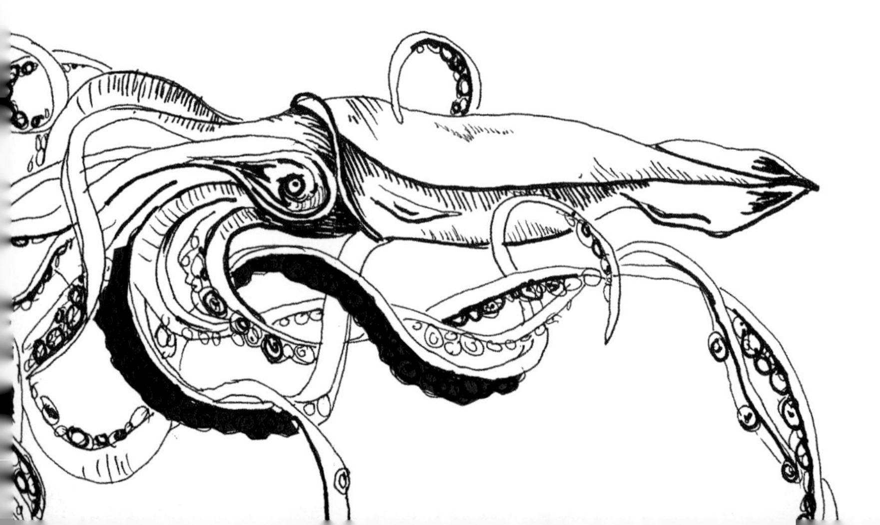

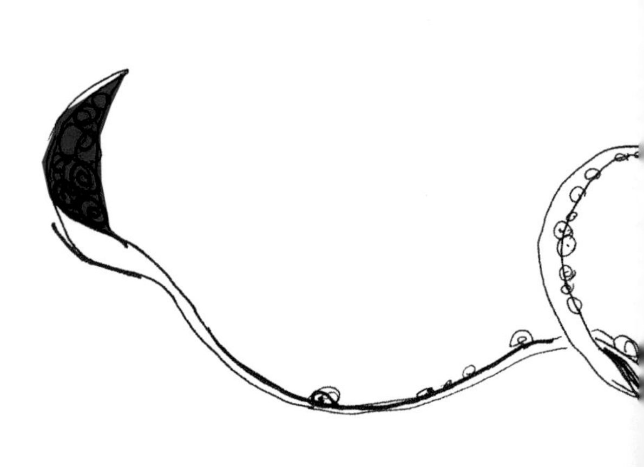

THE ROOT ROOM

SWEET STICKY BEETS

Serves 4-6

4-5 medium sized ***BEETROOT****, peeled and cut into 2cm chunky wedges*
3 cups (750ml) ***ORANGE JUICE***
3 tbsp ***HONEY***
2 tbsp ***BALSAMIC VINEGAR***
4 sprigs of ***FRESH THYME***
½ tsp ***SALT***
½ tsp freshly ***GROUND BLACK PEPPER***
1 cup ***FRESH MINT LEAVES***

Preheat oven to 180°C.

Partially cook the beetroot by placing in a saucepan covered with water. Bring to the boil and cook for 30 minutes. The water will reduce to almost nothing, so keep a close eye on it to prevent burning.

Combine the orange juice, honey, balsamic, thyme, salt, pepper and beetroot in a bowl.

Place the beetroot mix with its liquid in an oven dish. Roast for 30 minutes or until tender. When cooked, strain any remaining cooking juices into a saucepan and transfer the beetroot into a bowl. Reduce the liquid over a high heat for a few minutes to make a glaze.

Remove from the heat and set aside to cool.

To serve, toss the beetroot in the glaze with the fresh mint leaves.

Season with salt and pepper to taste.

MAPLE KUMARA, BACON & WALNUT

Serves 4-6

1kg ***KUMARA****, cut into 4cm cubes (peel if you like)*
⅓ cup (100g) ***MAPLE SYRUP***
2 tbsp ***OLIVE OIL***
SALT *and freshly* ***GROUND BLACK PEPPER***
4 rashers ***STREAKY BACON****, pan fried until crispy, roughly chopped*
1 cup (100g) ***WALNUTS****, toasted and roughly chopped (see pg 211)*
1 cup ***FRESH ITALIAN PARSLEY****, roughly chopped*
1 handful of ***BABY SPINACH LEAVES***
Drizzle of ***BALSAMIC VINEGAR***

Preheat oven to 180°C.

Line a shallow sided oven tray with baking paper. Add the chopped kumara and drizzle with maple syrup and olive oil. Season with salt and pepper. Toss well to coat.

Roast in the oven for 20 minutes. Turn the kumara and continue cooking for another 10 minutes or until golden. Remove from the oven and allow to cool.

In a large bowl, place the crispy bacon, toasted walnuts, parsley, spinach and roasted kumara, tossing gently to combine.

To serve, place on a platter, drizzle with a little balsamic vinegar and season with salt and pepper if necessary.

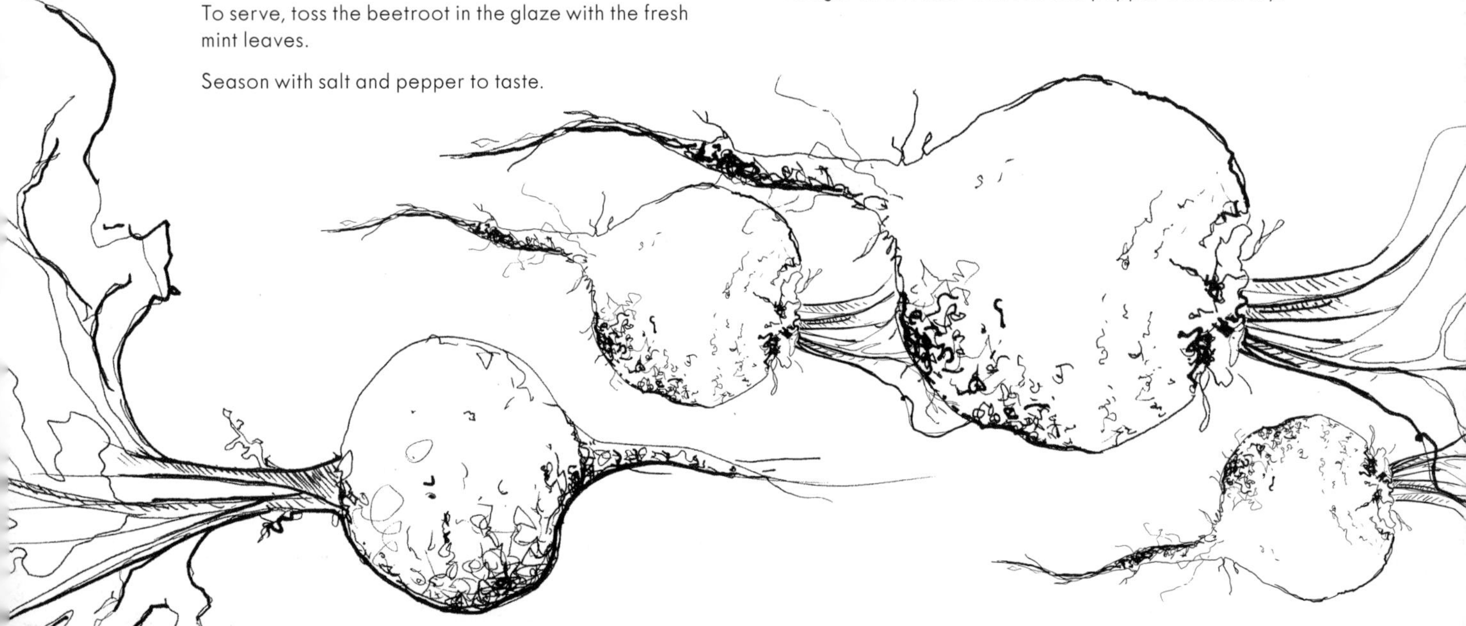

PUMPKIN, TAHINI & SEEDS

Serves 4-6

½ ***CROWN PUMPKIN****, de-seeded, cut into large 4cm thick wedges*
3 tbsp ***OLIVE OIL***
8-10 sprigs ***FRESH THYME,*** *leaves removed*
SALT *and freshly* **GROUND BLACK PEPPER**
3 tbsp ***PUMPKIN SEEDS***
1 cup ***TAHINI DRESSING*** *(see pg 204)*

Preheat oven to 180°C.

Lightly oil an oven tray and spread out the pumpkin wedges. Drizzle over the olive oil, thyme, salt and pepper and toss to coat.

Roast in a hot oven for 30-35 minutes. Add the seeds and cook for a further 10 minutes or until the pumpkin is tender when tested with a fork.

Place the cooked pumpkin and seeds onto a serving dish. Drizzle with tahini dressing and season to taste with salt and pepper.

MAORI POTATO & YAMS

Serves 4-6

80g ***BUTTER***
2 tbsp ***OLIVE OIL***
400g ***MAORI POTATOES****, "puri puri" sliced in half lengthways*
500g ***YAMS****, mixed colours, sliced in half lengthways*
200g new ***RED BABY POTATOES****, cut to a similar size if necessary*
1 ***WHOLE BULB GARLIC****, topped and tailed with skins left on*
5 ***WHOLE SHALLOTS****, skin left on*
2 ***FRESH CHILLIES****, finely sliced*
3 tbsp ***FRESH ROSEMARY LEAVES****, finely chopped*
3 ***FRESH ROSEMARY*** *sprigs*
1 tbsp ***SEA SALT***

Preheat oven to 180°C.

Place the butter and oil in a roasting pan and heat in the oven until bubbling, approximately 3 minutes.

Once the butter is hot, add all of the root vegetables, garlic, shallots, chilli, chopped and whole rosemary.

Roast together in the oven for 30 minutes. Remove roasting pan from oven and give a good shake. Add the salt and continue roasting until crunchy and golden.

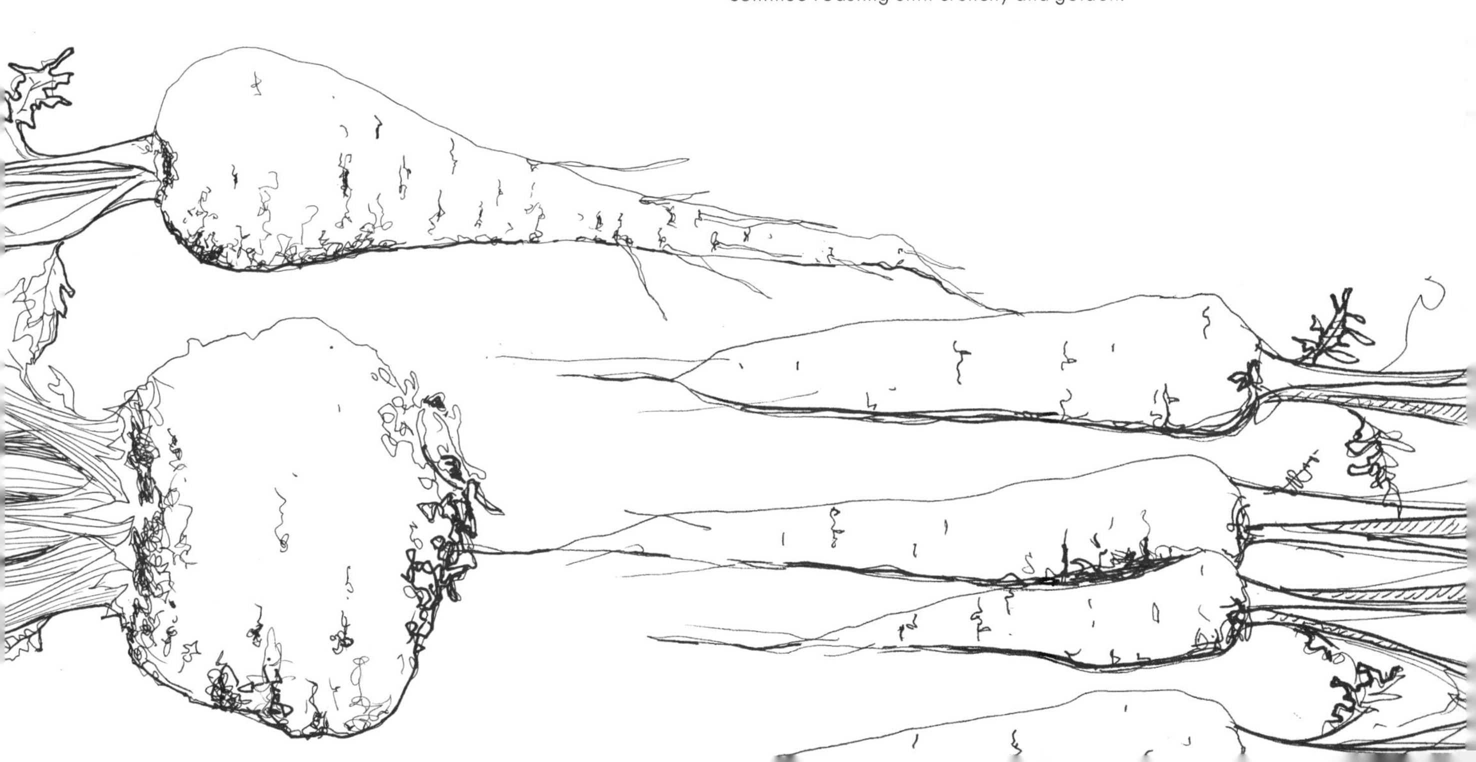

INDIAN SPICED CAULIFLOWER

Serves 4-6

1 cup ***CHICKPEAS****, soaked overnight*
¼ cup (60ml) ***VEGETABLE OIL***
2 ***ONIONS****, peeled, quartered and thinly sliced*
1½ tsp ***SALT***
1 tbsp ***CURRY POWDER***
2 tbsp ***CUMIN SEEDS***
1 tbsp ***GARAM MASALA***
1 tsp ***MUSTARD SEEDS***
1 tsp ***GROUND TURMERIC***
1 large ***CAULIFLOWER****, cut into 3cm florets*
2 tbsp ***SWEET CHILLI SAUCE***
2 cups ***FRESH CORIANDER LEAVES****, roughly chopped*
1 large handful of ***FRESH BABY SPINACH LEAVES***
JUICE *of 2* ***LEMONS***
JUICE *of 1* ***LIME***
SALT *and freshly* ***GROUND BLACK PEPPER***
1 cup of ***YOGHURT DRESSING*** *(see pg 204)*

Preheat oven to 180°C.

Cook chickpeas (see pg 210).

Heat the oil in a frying pan over a high heat. Add the onions and salt and cook until the onions are transparent, approximately 5 minutes. Add all the dry spices to the onion and cook for 2 minutes or until spices are fragrant.

Place the cauliflower florets into an oven roasting pan, add the cooked onion mix and lightly toss together.

Bake for 20-30minutes or until the cauliflower is tender to bite. Remove from the oven and allow to cool.

In a large bowl place the roasted cauliflower, sweet chilli sauce, fresh coriander leaves, baby spinach, chickpeas, lemon and lime juices. Toss gently and season with salt and pepper. Drizzle with yoghurt dressing to serve.

"Cauliflower is nothing but cabbage with a college education." – Mark Twain

ROASTED PARSNIP & SPICY LENTIL SALAD

Serves 4-6

1½ cups (300g) ***BROWN*** *or* ***GREEN LENTILS***
¼ cup (60ml) ***SWEET CHILLI SAUCE***
¼ cup (60ml) ***OLIVE OIL***
2 ***PARSNIPS****, peeled, trimmed and cut into 3, then cut lengthways*
1 medium ***CARROT****, peeled trimmed, cut into 3, then cut lengthways*
2 medium ***KUMARA****, peeled and cut into 2cm chunks*
1 tsp ***DRIED CHILLI FLAKES***
1 tbsp ***CURRY POWDER***
2 tsp ***CUMIN SEEDS***
2 tsp ***GROUND CUMIN***
½ cup ***FRESH ITALIAN PARSLEY***
½ cup ***FRESH CORIANDER LEAVES*** *or mint*
2 large handfuls of ***BABY SPINACH LEAVES***
JUICE *of ½ a* ***LEMON***
Drizzle of ***OLIVE OIL***
SALT *and freshly* ***GROUND BLACK PEPPER***
1 cup ***YOGHURT DRESSING*** *(see pg 204)*

Preheat oven to 180°C.

Cook the lentils (see pg 210).

In a small bowl mix together the sweet chilli sauce and olive oil.

Prepare the root vegetables and place in a bowl. Pour over the sweet chilli and oil, stirring to coat. Once an even coating is achieved transfer the vegetables to an oven tray for roasting.

In another small bowl combine the chilli flakes, curry powder, cumin seeds and ground cumin. Sprinkle this mixture over the vegetables and toss, ensuring that they are evenly coated.

Roast in oven for 40 minutes or until the vegetables have softened and are just starting to colour.

In another bowl, combine the cooked lentils, parsley, coriander and baby spinach. Dress with the lemon juice and olive oil.

Taste and season with salt and freshly ground black pepper if needed.

To assemble: alternate layers of the lentil and spinach mixture with the roasted vegetables.

Drizzle over the yoghurt dressing.

CUPCAKES

Cupcakes are always fun to make and eat. They are a great way to get the kids helping in the kitchen.

Try this recipe for a simple, satisfying treat. For a delicate high tea cupcake, remove the passion fruit pulp and add a piece of Turkish delight to the centre before baking. Decorate this version with pink icing and rose petals.

Feel free to halve this recipe if you are not catering for the masses, otherwise freeze a baked batch and defrost and decorate as needed.

Makes around 24

*375g **UNSALTED BUTTER**, melted*
*150g **CASTER SUGAR***
*100g soft **BROWN SUGAR***
*6 **EGGS***
*½ tsp **VANILLA EXTRACT***
*2 tbsp **MILK***
*375g **SELF RAISING FLOUR**, sifted*
*2 tbsp **PASSION FRUIT**, pulp*

Preheat oven to 180°C.

Line with paper patty cases or grease well, two 12 hole muffin or cupcake tins.

In a large mixing bowl, beat together the melted butter, caster sugar, brown sugar, eggs and vanilla until smooth.

Fold in the milk and flour in two stages. Finally, swirl in the passion fruit pulp. Spoon the mixture into the liners until they are ⅔ full.

Bake 20-25 minutes until they are a light golden brown and springy to the touch.

BUTTER CREAM ICING

Makes enough icing for 24 cupcakes, so remember to halve this recipe if you are doing the same with the cupcakes.

*100g **UNSALTED BUTTER**, softened*
*3 cups (480g) **ICING SUGAR**, sifted*
*¼ cup (60ml) **MILK**, approx*
*½ tsp **VANILLA EXTRACT***

In a mixing bowl cream the butter until it starts to get fluffy. Add the icing sugar, milk and vanilla, mixing until smooth. Add a little more milk, drop by drop, to achieve a good spreading consistency.

At this point let your creativity run wild with food colouring. Ice the cooled cupcakes and decorate.

CHOCOLATE BUTTER CREAM ICING

Again, this recipe makes enough icing for 24 cupcakes.

*100g **UNSALTED BUTTER**, softened*
*2¾ cups (440g) **ICING SUGAR***
*¼ cup (25g) **COCOA***
*¼ cup (60ml) **MILK**, approx*
*½ tsp **VANILLA EXTRACT***

Follow the same method as the butter cream recipe, adding the cocoa with the icing sugar.

OATY GINGER SLICE

BASE

200g ***UNSALTED BUTTER****, cubed*
3 tbsp ***GOLDEN SYRUP***
1 cup (160g) soft ***BROWN SUGAR***
1 cup (100g) ***DESICCATED COCONUT***
2 cups (200g) ***ROLLED OATS***
1 cup (150g) ***FLOUR***
2 tsp ***BAKING POWDER***
2 tsp ***GROUND GINGER***

TOPPING

2 tbsp ***GOLDEN SYRUP***
75g ***UNSALTED BUTTER***
1 cup (160g) ***ICING SUGAR***
1 tbsp ***GROUND GINGER***

Preheat oven to 170°C.

Grease and line a 20 x 30cm slice tin with baking paper.

To prepare the base: in a saucepan over a low to medium heat melt the butter, golden syrup and brown sugar. Stir until combined and the sugar has dissolved.

In a large bowl mix the coconut, rolled oats, flour, baking powder and ginger. Pour the melted butter mixture over and thoroughly combine. Press into the lined slice tin and bake for 20 minutes or until golden.

Remove from the oven and mark into squares, not quite the whole way through. Do this when the base is still warm, as it's easier to cut at this stage. Allow to cool.

To prepare the topping: melt the golden syrup and butter together in a saucepan. Sift the icing sugar and ginger into the saucepan and with a wooden spoon beat the topping until smooth. Spread with a spatula over the cooled base while the icing is still hot.

Allow the slice to cool and then gently break the pieces apart.

GREEK COCONUT & LEMON SYRUP CAKE

Monique Dentice introduced this wonderful recipe to Ripe. It's an impressive looking cake and although there are three stages to the recipe the effort is definitely worth it.

Serves 8-10

CAKE

250g ***UNSALTED BUTTER****, softened*

2 cups (440g) ***CASTER SUGAR***

6 ***EGGS***

2 cups (300g) plain ***FLOUR***

2 tsp ***BAKING POWDER***

1 cup (100g) ***DESICCATED COCONUT***

1 cup (280g) ***SOUR CREAM*** *or natural yoghurt*

CITRUS SYRUP

2 cups (500ml) ***WATER***

1 cup (220g) ***WHITE SUGAR***

ZEST *of 1* ***ORANGE***

ZEST *of 1* ***LEMON***

1 cup (250ml) ***ORANGE*** *or* ***LEMON JUICE***

MERINGUE TOPPING

6 ***EGG WHITES***

1 tbsp ***CASTER SUGAR***

1½ cups (100g) ***LONG THREAD COCONUT***

⅓ cup (110g) ***RASPBERRY JAM****, to serve*

Preheat oven to 180°C.

Grease and line the base and sides of a 26cm spring form tin with baking paper.

To prepare the cake: place the softened butter and caster sugar in a large bowl. Cream together until light and pale in colour.

Add the eggs one at a time, beating well after each addition. Gently fold in the flour and baking powder to combine. Lastly, fold in the coconut and sour cream or yoghurt until combined.

Pour the cake mix into the prepared tin and bake for 50-60 minutes or until a skewer inserted into the centre comes out clean. Remove the cake from the oven and keep the oven heated to 180°C. With a skewer, poke holes into the surface of the cooked cake while it's still hot and in its tin.

To prepare the syrup: combine all the syrup ingredients in a saucepan over a medium heat. Stir until the sugar has dissolved and the liquid has reduced slightly.

Pour the citrus syrup over the cake.

To prepare the topping: whisk the egg whites until stiff peaks form then slowly add the sugar (see pg 208).

Very gently, fold in the long thread coconut and spread topping over the top of the cake.

Bake until the meringue has turned golden. This should take approximately 15 minutes.

Remove from the oven and swirl over the raspberry jam. Finally, cool in the tin before removing the cake.

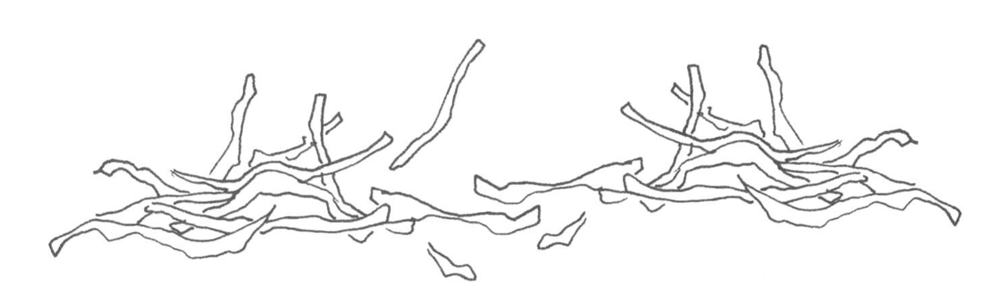

HOT CHOCOLATE MOUSSE PUDDING

This pudding is one you will want to make again and again. It's cakey, moussy and saucy! Bob Dylan loves it too!

It's also wheat and gluten free. A great dessert for all ages. Thank you Amy Melchior for sharing this recipe.

As this is a mousse, you can't cook it ahead of time, so we would advise that if you are having a dinner party get everything ready in advance, eg. chocolate melted and kept warm, egg whites whipped.

Just before serving your main course, fold the egg whites into the chocolate and bake the mousse so it cooks while you and your guests are enjoying your meal. It will happily sit for 10-15 minutes between leaving the oven and serving.

Serves 6

*400g **DARK CHOCOLATE**, 72% cocoa*
*200g **UNSALTED BUTTER***
*9 large **EGGS**, separated*
*100g soft **BROWN SUGAR***
*120g **CASTER SUGAR***
*1 **VANILLA POD**, or 1 tsp of vanilla extract*
*A pinch of **SALT***

Preheat oven to 180°C.

Use a deep sided ovenproof dish, approximately 20 x 20cm. This dessert works in most dishes around this size.

Place a heatproof bowl over a pot of simmering water. Melt the chocolate and butter together in the bowl (see pg 207).

In another bowl, whisk the egg yolks, the sugars, vanilla and salt until the mixture reaches a creamy, mayonnaise like consistency. This takes a few minutes of rapid beating by hand.

In a dry bowl, whisk the egg whites until they reach a soft peak consistency. With a large metal spoon gently fold the melted chocolate and butter into the yolks and sugar. Introduce the egg whites to the mix by combining a single tablespoonful first. This helps to protect the air in the whites while you mix. Once incorporated, gently fold in the remaining egg whites.

Pour the mixture into the ovenproof dish and bake for 25-30 minutes or until just set on the surface. It will still seem quite wobbly but this is good – think soufflé!

Serve while warm with runny or whipped cream.

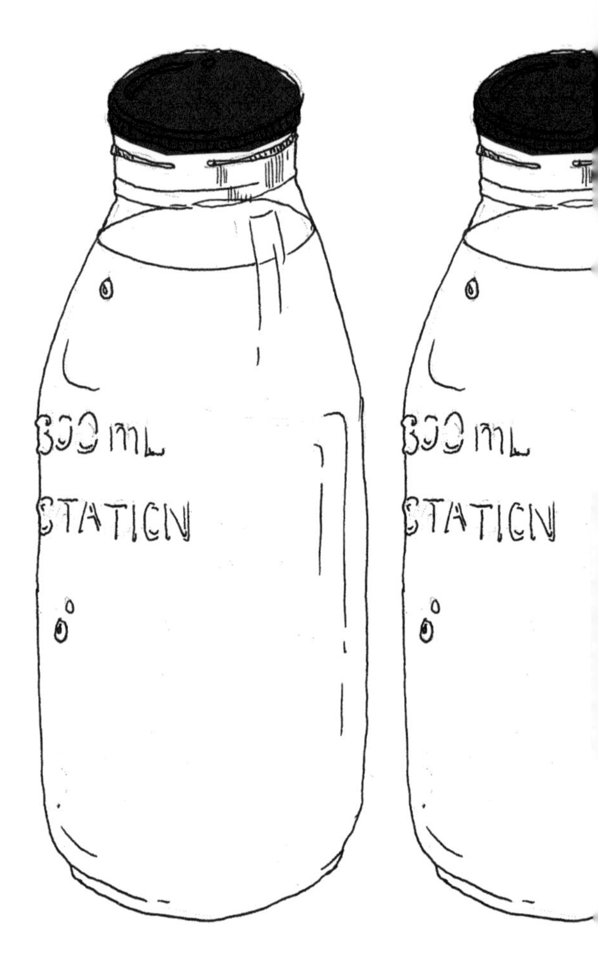

"My wife dresses to kill – she cooks the same way." – Henry Youngman

Beetroot. Cabbages. Cauliflower. Carrots. Broccolini. Citrus. Leeks. Parsnips. Swedes. Tamarillos. Yams. Avocado. Broad beans. Brussel sprouts. Celery. Kale. Rhubarb. Spinach. Turnips.

AUGUST I SEPTEMBER

Citrus is abundant during these months.
It's a great time for making lemon honey or preserving lemons and limes.

RIPE TOASTED MUESLI

We have this available every day at Ripe and it is a favourite of our many dedicated locals. We even have a customer who gets it posted to him regularly in Paris. Served with fruit salad and your favourite yoghurt, you're guaranteed a good start to the day.

Makes around 2kg

1kg quick cook ***OATS***
180g ***LONG THREAD COCONUT***
180g ***SESAME SEEDS***
150g ***BAKING BRAN***
100g ***WHEAT GERM***
125g ***PECANS****, chopped*
100g ***ALMONDS****, sliced*
200ml ***LIQUID HONEY***
200ml ***RICE BRAN OIL***
250g ***CURRANTS***
200g ***DRIED APRICOTS****, roughly chopped*

Preheat oven to 160°C,

In a large bowl mix the oats, coconut, sesame seeds, bran, wheat germ and nuts. In another bowl combine the honey and oil. Pour over the dry ingredients and stir until coated. Spread the mixture onto a large oven roasting tray and place in the oven.

Every 10 minutes or so check the muesli and give it a stir to toast it evenly. Continue until all the muesli is toasted and golden brown. This could take up to 40 minutes. Remove from the oven and once it has cooled a little, add the dried fruit.

Stir together well and break up any clusters before storing in an air tight container.

WINTER COMPOTE

This is fantastic in winter when the choice of seasonal fruit is comparatively low.

Serve the compote with muesli or gingerbread.

Experiment and select your favourite dried fruit. It stores well in the fridge, so you may want to double up the recipe.

2 cups ***DRIED FRUIT*** *– prunes, figs, and apricots work well*
3 cups (750ml) ***WATER***
JUICE *and* ***ZEST*** *of 1* ***ORANGE***
1 whole ***CINNAMON STICK***
2 whole ***STAR ANISE***
1 ***PEAR****, sliced (optional)*
1 cup ***BERRIES****, frozen (optional)*

Place the dried fruit in a saucepan. Add the water, orange juice and zest, cinnamon stick and star anise.

Cook on a medium heat and simmer until the water is nearly absorbed, approximately 10-15 minutes.

It's really tasty with 1 whole pear, thinly sliced, or 1 cup of frozen berries added near the end of cooking time.

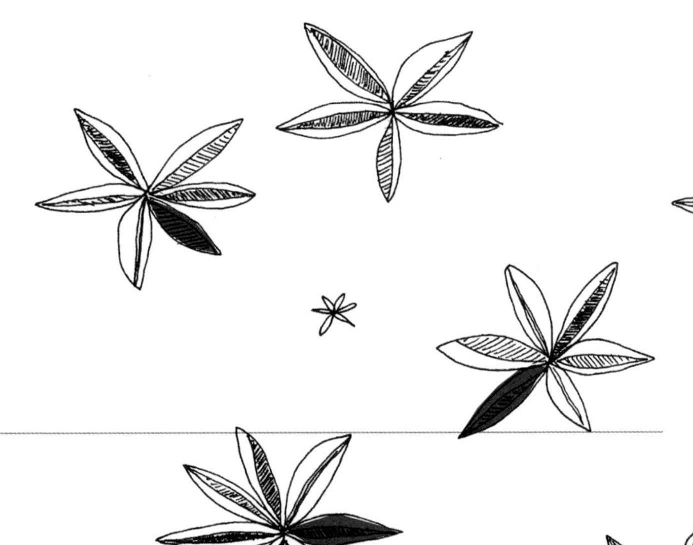

CURRIED PARSNIP & APPLE SOUP

Serves 4-6

1 tbsp ***OLIVE OIL***
1 ***ONION****, peeled, roughly chopped*
2 cloves ***GARLIC****, peeled and crushed*
1 tsp ***MUSTARD SEEDS***
1 tsp ***GROUND CUMIN***
1 tsp ***FRESH GINGER****, peeled and finely chopped*
1 tbsp ***CURRY POWDER***
4 large ***PARSNIPS****, peeled and roughly chopped*
2 ***APPLES****, cored, peeled and roughly chopped*
4 cups (1ltr) ***CHICKEN STOCK***
1 tbsp soft ***BROWN SUGAR***
1 tbsp ***BUTTER***
¼ cup (60ml) ***CREAM***
SALT *and freshly* ***GROUND BLACK PEPPER***

Heat the oil in a large saucepan over a medium heat. Add the onion and garlic, cooking for 2 minutes.

Add the spices and cook for a further 2 minutes to draw out the flavours. Add the parsnips, apple and chicken stock and stir to combine.

Cook for approximately 30 minutes until the parsnips and apple are soft. Add the brown sugar, butter and cream and continue to cook for a few minutes.

Blend with a stick blender until smooth.

Season with salt and pepper to taste.

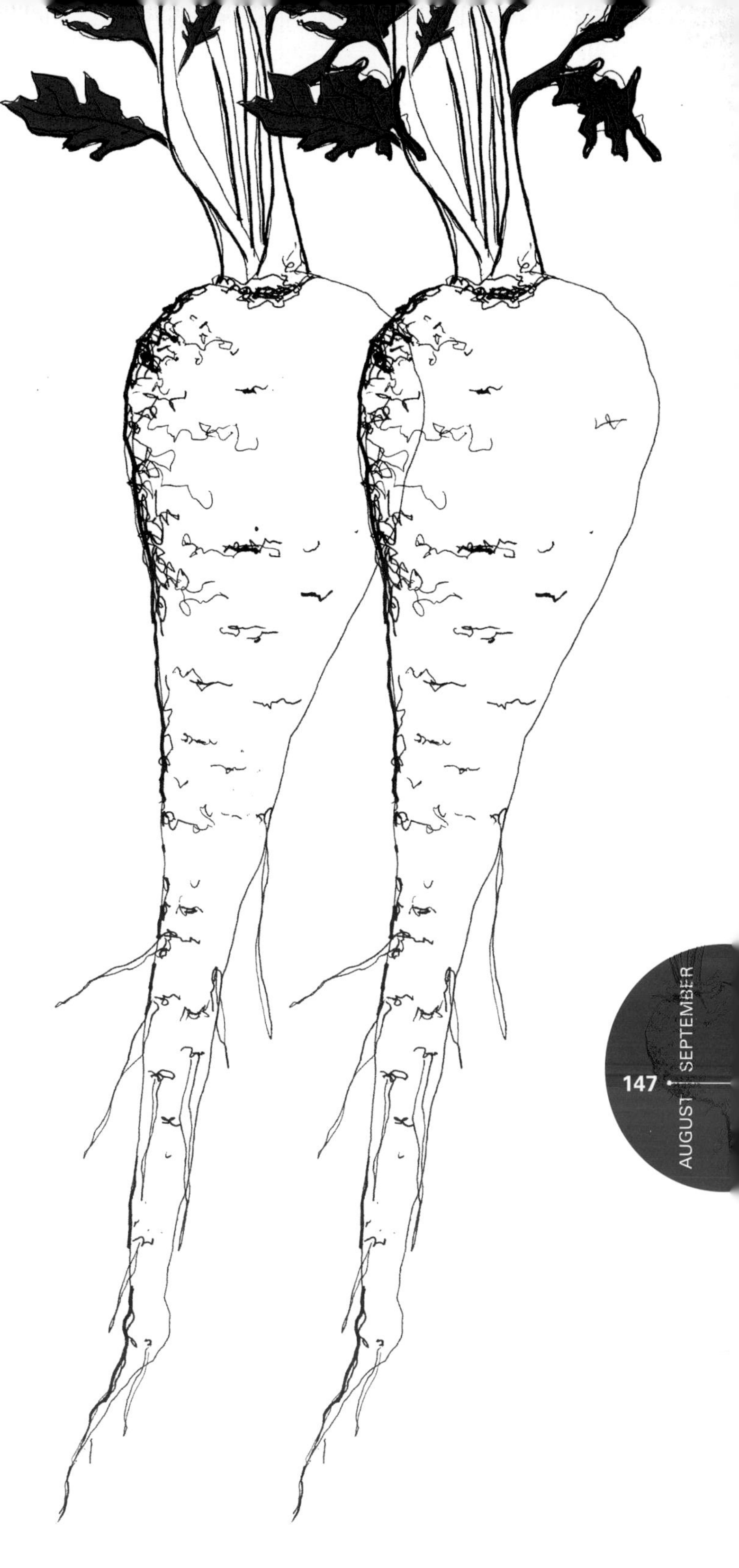

"My mother's menu consisted of two choices... Take it or leave it." – Buddy Hackett

HARIRA

A delicious Moroccan soup that is a hearty meal in itself. This recipe does make a large quantity but it freezes well.

Serves 6-8

½ cup (100g) ***CHICKPEAS****, soaked overnight*
2 tbsp ***BUTTER***
1 tbsp ***OIL***
500g ***LAMB****, cut into 1cm cubes*
6 cloves ***GARLIC****, peeled, crushed and finely sliced*
2 ***CARROTS****, peeled and roughly chopped into 1cm cubes*
2 ***ONIONS****, peeled, diced*
2 ***CELERY*** *stalks, diced, leaves included*
1 tbsp ***GROUND CUMIN***
1 ***CINNAMON STICK***
1 tbsp ***CORIANDER SEEDS****, ground*
1 tbsp ***GROUND GINGER***
1 tbsp ***GROUND TURMERIC***
3 x 400g can ***CRUSHED TOMATOES***
¾ cup (150g) ***PUY LENTILS***
6 cups (1½ltr) ***CHICKEN STOCK***
1 cup ***FRESH ITALIAN PARSLEY****, roughly chopped*
2 tsp ***SALT***
½ cup ***DRIED ANGEL HAIR PASTA****, or fine spaghetti broken into small pieces*
4 ***FRESH TOMATOES****, roughly chopped*
1 cup ***FRESH CORIANDER LEAVES****, roughly chopped*
JUICE *of 1* ***LEMON***
Freshly ***GROUND BLACK PEPPER***

Cook chickpeas (see pg 210).

In a large saucepan over a medium heat melt the butter and oil. Add the lamb, garlic, carrots, onions, celery, cumin, cinnamon stick, coriander seeds, ginger and turmeric and fry for 10 minutes.

Add the crushed tomatoes, lentils and chicken stock and bring to the boil.

Reduce the heat and simmer for 1½ hours or until the lamb is tender.

Add the parsley, chickpeas, salt, pasta, fresh tomato, coriander and lemon juice. Cook gently for a further 10 minutes or until the pasta is tender.

Season with salt and pepper to taste. Serve with loads of fresh pide (Turkish) bread.

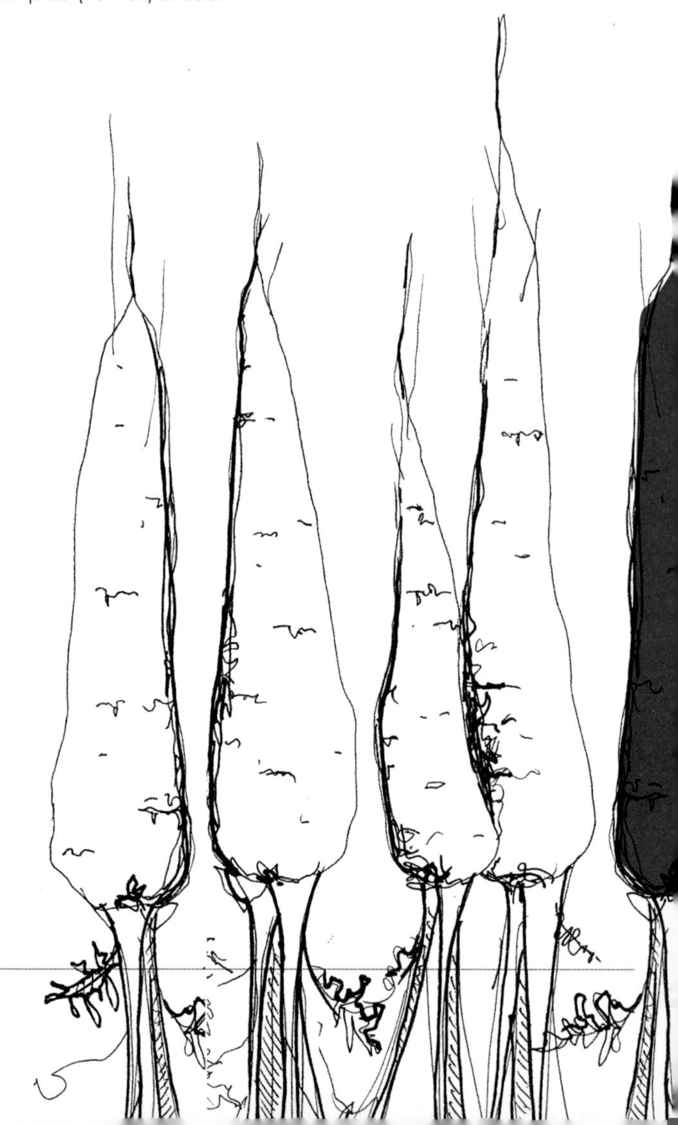

RED BEAN PATTIES

John Utumapu is a real team player. He is always going out of his way to help everyone. John creates some great dishes at Ripe. This is one of our favourites.

By all means, play around with bean varieties – even tinned beans work well.

They taste even better accompanied by the spicy tomato relish (see pg 82), and are great served with "Cole" slaw from the Slaw Floor (see pg 192).

Serves 6-8

1 cup (200g) **CANNELLINI BEANS**, *soaked overnight*
½ cup (100g) **KIDNEY BEANS**, *soaked overnight*
1 tbsp **CUMIN SEEDS**, *toasted (see pg 211)*
1 tbsp **CORIANDER SEEDS**, *toasted*
1 tsp **GROUND CARDAMOM**
¼ tsp **GROUND CLOVES**
1 tbsp **OLIVE OIL**
½ **ONION**, *peeled, finely diced*
3 cloves **GARLIC**, *peeled and finely sliced*
3cm piece **FRESH GINGER**, *peeled and grated*
150g **FRESH SPINACH LEAVES**
½ cup **FRESH ITALIAN PARSLEY**, *roughly chopped*
1 cup **FRESH CORIANDER LEAVES**, *roughly chopped*
1 tbsp **BALSAMIC VINEGAR**
1 cup (100g) dried **BREAD CRUMBS** *+ extra for crumbing*
1 **EGG**, *lightly beaten*
¼ cup **SPICY TOMATO RELISH** *(see pg 82) or tomato sauce.*
1 tsp **SALT**
1 tsp freshly **GROUND BLACK PEPPER**
VEGETABLE OIL *for frying*
1 handful of **SPINACH** *leaves, blanched (optional for serving)*

Cook beans (see pg 210).

In a mortar and pestle combine the cumin, coriander, cardamom and cloves and grind well.

Place the beans in a food processer bowl and pulse until chunky.

In a small frying pan, heat the oil. Once hot, add the ground spices and stir continuously for 1 minute until aromatic. Add the onion, garlic and ginger and continue to cook for 5 minutes or until the onion is translucent.

Remove from the heat and transfer to a bowl. Allow to cool.

Boil a little water in a frying pan. Add the spinach and cook until it is wilted, approximately 1 minute. Drain off any excess water and squeeze dry.

Into the food processor bowl (with the beans), add the onion and spice mixture, blanched spinach, parsley, coriander, balsamic vinegar, bread crumbs, egg, tomato relish, salt and pepper.

Pulse the processor to combine the mixture. Place the pattie mixture into the fridge for 30 minutes to chill, as it will be too soft to shape. When chilled shape into patties and roll in the bread crumbs to lightly coat.

Preheat oven to 180°C.

Over a medium heat in a large frying pan, heat a dash of oil and cook the patties on either side for 2 minutes.

Transfer the patties to an oven dish and bake for 15 minutes.

Optional: when serving, wrap each patty in a spinach leaf and add a dollop of tomato relish on top.

TAMARIND & TEMPEH CURRY

Tempeh is an Indonesian fermented soya bean cake that looks and sounds odd, but tastes nutty (almost like cashews) and is very good for you. You will find it in health food shops or your favourite Asian supermarket.

Make sure you use a Thai tamarind pulp, the Indian one is more like molasses and is not suitable for this recipe. If you like a sweet curry, you'll love this one!

Serves 4-6

TAMARIND SAUCE

450ml of Thai ***TAMARIND PULP***
¾ cup ***PALM SUGAR****, grated or ¾ cup soft brown sugar*
1 cup (250ml) ***WATER***

TEMPEH CURRY

2 tbsp ***VEGETABLE OIL***
1 ***ONION****, peeled, finely sliced*
6 cloves ***GARLIC****, crushed, roughly chopped*
4 tsp (2cm piece) ***FRESH GINGER****, peeled and grated*
3 fresh ***RED CHILLIES****, de-seeded and finely sliced*
5 KAFFIR LIME LEAVES*, roughly torn*
1 block (300g) of ***TEMPEH*** *or firm tofu chopped into eighths*
1 ***GOLDEN KUMARA*** *or potato, peeled, chopped into 2cm cubes*
1 ***EGGPLANT*** *chopped into 2cm cubes*
4 cups (1ltr) ***VEGETABLE STOCK***
1 cup ***TAMARIND SAUCE*** *(SEE BELOW)*
1 cup (250ml) ***WATER***
1 bunch of ***ASIAN GREENS*** *or bok choy*
1 bunch of ***BROCCOLINI****, roughly chopped*
200g ***GREEN BEANS****, topped and tailed*
SALT *and freshly* ***GROUND BLACK PEPPER***
3 ripe ***BANANAS***
1 tbsp ***VEGETABLE OIL***
3 tbsp soft ***BROWN SUGAR***
¼ cup ***FRESH CORIANDER LEAVES****, roughly chopped*
½ cup (125ml) ***COCONUT CREAM*** *(optional)*

To prepare the tamarind sauce: place the tamarind pulp, sugar and water in a small saucepan and bring to the boil, stirring until the tamarind pulp and sugar have dissolved and it is starting to thicken.

Use half of the tamarind sauce for the curry and save the remainder for another day. It will store for months in the fridge. Use up any extra as a marinade for fish, chicken, beef or duck.

To prepare the tempeh curry: in a large saucepan over a high heat, combine the oil, onion, garlic, ginger, chillies, lime leaves and tempeh. Cook for 5 minutes or until the onion is just starting to colour. Add the kumara and eggplant and cook for a further 5 minutes.

Add the vegetable stock, tamarind sauce and water. Bring to the boil, reduce the heat and allow to simmer for 15 minutes.

Mix in the Asian greens, broccolini and beans. Cook for a few minutes or until the broccolini is tender. Season with salt and freshly ground black pepper.

Peel and slice the bananas lengthways.

Bring a frying pan to a high heat and add the vegetable oil. Place the bananas into the frying pan and sprinkle with brown sugar. Fry the bananas without moving them for a minute then gently turn them over and cook the other side.

Serve the curry on a bed of rice, topped with the fresh coriander leaves and cooked bananas.

Pour over a little coconut cream if desired.

LAO GREEN CUCUMBER SALAD WITH STICKY RICE

This is a truly wonderful recipe from Amy Melchior. Amy has been a huge part of the success of Ripe. As well as being a very talented chef she is a gifted full-time artist specialising in encaustic painting. Keep an eye out for her exhibitions.

"This recipe really is a party of flavours in your mouth," says Amy.

Serves 4-6

LAO GREEN CUCUMBER SALAD

4 **TELEGRAPH CUCUMBERS**
4 cloves **GARLIC**, peeled and roughly chopped
4 tsp (2cm piece) **FRESH GINGER**, peeled and grated
2 tsp **DRIED SHRIMPS**
3-4 fresh **RED CHILLIES**, deseed if you want to lower the heat
2 tbsp **PALM SUGAR**, grated
2-3 tsp Thai **FISH SAUCE**
3 **LIMES**, peeled and quartered
1 x 250g punnet **CHERRY TOMATOES**, halved
200g **GREEN BEANS** (snake beans if available), roughly chopped
1 cup **FRESH CORIANDER LEAVES**, roughly chopped
1 cup **FRESH MINT LEAVES**, roughly chopped
½ cup (80g) **ROASTED UNSALTED PEANUTS**
½ **ICEBERG LETTUCE** head, shredded (optional)

To prepare the salad: peel the cucumber, cut in half lengthways and scrape out and discard the seeds with a teaspoon. Julienne (cut into long strips), then set aside in a bowl and refrigerate.

In a large mortar and pestle place the garlic, ginger, dried shrimp, chilli and palm sugar. Pound gently until you have a paste.

Add the fish sauce, lime pieces and pound gently again. If there is enough room in your mortar, add the tomatoes and beans. Otherwise transfer to a metal bowl and pound until the beans and tomatoes are smashed up and the flavours have mixed together.

In a large serving bowl place the cucumber, the pounded mixture, coriander, mint, peanuts and shredded iceberg lettuce and toss together. Serve with the sticky rice.

STICKY RICE

Not like any other rice, this rice is super-glutinous. You can find it at any Asian supermarket – remember to ask for the special little basket you need to cook it in. Please note the sticky rice needs soaking overnight.

2 cups **WHITE GLUTINOUS RICE**

To prepare the sticky rice: soak the rice overnight in plenty of water. Drain and rinse.

Place the rice into the basket then into a saucepan. Add a small amount of water until it sits just under the base of the basket, but not touching.

Place the saucepan on a medium heat and steam the rice. You may need to check the water level and top up during the 20-30 minutes of steaming needed to cook the rice. The rice will be glossy and sticky when ready.

This may seem arduous but it is really worth the sensation of fresh sticky rice and cucumber salad.

If it's all too much, just serve the cucumber salad with freshly cooked basmati rice!

BUTTER CHICKEN, RAITA & PILAF

A wonderful recipe from Thereza D'Souza who worked as a chef at Ripe. This keeps well in the freezer and makes a great pie filling too.

Serves 4

CHICKEN MARINADE

500g skinless ***CHICKEN THIGH*** *or skinless breast meat, diced*
½ cup (140g) ***UNSWEETENED NATURAL YOGHURT***
2 tsp (1cm piece) ***FRESH GINGER****, grated*
6 CLOVES GARLIC*, peeled, finely chopped*
1 tsp ***GARAM MASALA***
¼ tsp ***CHILLI POWDER***
1 tsp ***SALT***

SAUCE

A dash of ***OIL***
1 ***ONION****, peeled, finely chopped*
50g ***CASHEW NUTS****, toasted* *(see pg 211)*
¼ cup (60ml) ***VEGETABLE OIL***
1 tsp ***GARAM MASALA***
¼ tsp ***CHILLI POWDER***
1 ***CINNAMON STICK***
1 tsp ***CORIANDER SEEDS***
1 whole ***CARDAMOM POD***
1 tsp ***CUMIN SEEDS***
3 ***WHOLE CLOVES***
100g ***TOMATO PASTE***
100ml ***CREAM***
1 cup (250ml) ***CHICKEN STOCK***
2 tsp ***WHITE SUGAR***
2 tsp ***SALT***
50g ***BUTTER***

Preheat oven to 180°C.

To prepare the marinade: put the chicken and all the marinade ingredients in a large bowl or sealable plastic bag. Mix well to coat the chicken and chill for at least 1 hour.

Place the marinated chicken into a deep sided ovenproof dish and cook until the juices run clear, approximately 30 minutes.

To prepare the sauce: place a large frying pan over a medium heat and add a dash of oil. Cook the onion until softened and just beginning to colour. Set aside to cool.

Place the fried onions and cashews in a mortar and pestle or blender and pound together to make a paste.

Place vegtable oil in a frying pan on a medium to low heat. Add the garam masala, chilli powder, cinnamon stick, coriander seeds, whole cardamom, cumin seeds, cloves and tomato paste and cook for 5 minutes.

Add the cooked chicken and juices, cream, stock, onion and cashew paste. Mix well. Taste and season with the sugar and salt. Continue cooking for a further 10 minutes. Finally, add the butter stirring to combine.

Serve with plain fluffy rice and raita or with the flavourful pilaf (see below).

RAITA

Makes approx 2 cups | Serves 4-6

½ ***TELEGRAPH CUCUMBER****, halved and de-seeded*
1 cup (280g) ***UNSWEETENED NATURAL YOGHURT***
¼ cup ***FRESH MINT LEAVES****, chopped*
SALT *and freshly* ***GROUND BLACK PEPPER***

Into a bowl, grate the de-seeded cucumber and sprinkle with a large pinch of salt. Set aside for 10 minutes.

Rinse the cucumber under cold running water. Strain and squeeze the excess liquid out with your hands.

In a bowl, mix together the yoghurt, mint and cucumber. Season with salt and pepper to taste.

PILAF

2 ***ONIONS**, peeled and finely sliced*
*50g **BUTTER***
*4 whole **CARDAMOM PODS**, smashed*
*1 **CINNAMON STICK***
*1 tbsp **CUMIN SEEDS***
*1½ cups (300g) **BASMATI RICE***
*1 cup **MIXED DRIED FRUIT**, roughly chopped*
*3 cups (750ml) **WATER***
*¼ cup **FRESH MINT LEAVES**, finely chopped*
SALT** and freshly **GROUND BLACK PEPPER

In a large saucepan over a medium to high heat, add the onions and butter. Stir and fry for 1 minute. Then cover with a lid and cook until golden and tender, approximately 5 minutes. Add the cardamom, cinnamon, cumin, rice and dried fruit. Cook for 2-3 minutes. Lastly add the water and bring to the boil.

Cover with a lid and simmer on a low heat for 10 minutes. Remove from the heat and leave to stand for 15 minutes. Lightly fluff the grains with a fork and add the fresh mint leaves. Season to taste with salt and pepper.

BEEF DAUBE

This is traditionally cooked in a daubiere, which is a glazed earthenware pot with a tightly fitting lid. Choose a deep heavy casserole dish for best results. Delicious with our Creamy Polenta (see pg 161) and Cabbage and Caraway from The Green Room (see pg 162).

Serves 6-8

*1kg **BEEF CHUCK STEAK**, cut into 2-3cm pieces*
*¼ cup (40g) plain **FLOUR**, seasoned with salt and pepper*
*¼ cup (60ml) **OLIVE OIL***
*2 small **ONIONS**, peeled, roughly chopped*
*6 cloves **GARLIC**, peeled and thinly sliced*
*225g **STREAKY BACON**, cut into strips*
*2 stalks **CELERY**, sliced into chunks*
*¼ cup (60ml) **RED WINE VINEGAR***
*2 cups (500ml) **RED WINE***
*2 small **CARROTS**, peeled and chunkily sliced*
*2 **BAY LEAVES**, torn*
*2 sprigs **FRESH THYME***
*½ tsp **GROUND CINNAMON***
*2 cups (500ml) **BEEF STOCK***
*2 cups (500ml) **WATER***
*½ tsp freshly **GROUND BLACK PEPPER***
*½ cup (80g) **KALAMATA OLIVES***

Preheat oven to 180°C.

Toss the beef pieces in the seasoned flour to gain a light coating. Dust off the excess.

In a large frying pan over a medium heat, heat half the olive oil until just starting to smoke. Brown the beef, a few pieces at a time, turning once with tongs. Remove from the heat and transfer to a large casserole dish.

Using the same frying pan, add the remaining olive oil and heat it to smoking point again. Add the onions, garlic, bacon and celery and cook for 2-3 minutes over a medium heat. Remove the pan from the heat and add the mixture to the casserole dish with the meat.

Deglaze the pan by bringing it up to a high heat and adding the red wine vinegar and red wine (see pg 209). Stir and bring it to a rapid boil, which will take approximately 30 seconds. Pour the liquid over the meat and vegetables in the casserole dish.

Finally, add directly to the casserole dish the carrots, bay leaves, thyme, cinnamon, beef stock, water and freshly ground black pepper.

Cover the casserole dish and place in the hot oven for 2½ hours, or until the meat is very tender.

Stir through the olives just before serving.

GOATS' CHEESE GRATIN

By all means add other root vegetables such as kumara or parsnip. Change the ratio of cream and stock if you are after a lower calorie dish.

Serves 4-6

*4-5 large sized **POTATOES**, peeled, thinly sliced lengthways*
*2 sprigs **FRESH ROSEMARY**, leaves picked and finely chopped*
*1 **RED ONION**, peeled and thinly sliced*
*2 cups (500ml) **CREAM***
*1 cup (250ml) **VEGETABLE** or chicken **STOCK***
*½ tsp **SALT***
*½ tsp freshly **GROUND BLACK PEPPER***
*150g **GOATS' CHEESE***
*3 tbsp **FRESH ITALIAN PARSLEY**, roughly chopped*

Preheat oven to 180°C. Grease a lasagne style ovenproof dish with a little butter.

In a large bowl combine the potatoes, fresh rosemary and red onion. Pour over the cream, stock, salt and pepper, mixing well to coat the potato slices. Pour the potato mixture into the baking dish, arranging the slices of potato and pressing down lightly. Cover with tin foil and bake for 1 hour.

Take out of the oven, remove the foil and crumble over the goats' cheese. Sprinkle on the parsley and season with extra pepper. Return to the oven for 10-15 minutes or until the cheese is just starting to colour.

"I cook with wine, sometimes I even add it to the food." – W. C. Fields

S&M AND SAUCE

Sausages and Mash, the ultimate favourite for all ages. We have chosen a couple of our favourite mashes. Mix and match your favourite sausage, mash and gravy combo. Any combination is sure to be a hit!

SAUSAGES

After much consultation, here are the best two ways we've found to cook your favourite sausages.

PAR-BOILED AND PAN FRIED (GOOD FOR THICKER SAUSAGES)

Place a saucepan of water on to boil and add the sausages. Simmer for 5 minutes then remove and drain well. Dry with kitchen paper.

Place a frying pan on a high heat with a splash of oil. Add the sausages and cook until golden brown.

BAKED

Preheat oven to 200°C.

Line a small oven tray and cook the sausages in the oven until golden brown.

"Hunger is the best sauce." – proverb

MASHES

CHAMP

Famous Irish mash.

Serves 4

*1kg floury **POTATOES**, peeled and cut into large pieces – Agria work well*
*60g **BUTTER***
*¾ cup (180ml) **CREAM**, or milk, or a combination*
*1 tsp **SALT***
*Freshly **GROUND BLACK PEPPER***
*4 **SPRING ONIONS**, ends trimmed and thinly sliced*

In a large saucepan cover the potatoes with water. Cover the pan and bring to the boil. After 15-20 minutes check if the potatoes are cooked by spearing with a fork.

Drain well and mash with a good old fashioned masher. Add the butter, cream, salt and pepper and stir to combine. Add more liquid if required for a creamy consistency. Finally stir in the spring onions.

KUMARA, POTATO & GARLIC MASH

Serves 4

*500g floury **POTATOES**, peeled and chopped into large pieces – Agria work well*
*500g **KUMARA**, peeled and chopped into large pieces*
*10 cloves **GARLIC**, peeled*
*60g **BUTTER***
*½ cup (125ml) **CREAM** or milk*
*1 tsp **SALT***
*Freshly **GROUND BLACK PEPPER***
*1 tbsp **FRESH ITALIAN PARSLEY**, finely chopped*

In a large saucepan cover the potatoes, kumara and garlic with water.

Bring to the boil and cook for 15-20 minutes until soft. Drain well and mash with a good old fashioned masher. Add the butter, cream, salt and pepper.

Fold the fresh herbs in just before serving.

CREAMY POLENTA

Serves 6

4 cups (1ltr) ***CHICKEN*** *or vegetable* ***STOCK***
1 cup (250ml) ***CREAM***
½ tsp ***SALT***
½ tsp freshly ***GROUND BLACK PEPPER***
1 tbsp ***FRESH THYME LEAVES****, finely chopped*
1 cup (160g) instant ***POLENTA***
½ cup (40g) ***PARMESAN****, grated*

In a medium saucepan heat the stock, cream, salt, pepper and the fresh thyme.

Bring to the boil. Slowly whisk in the polenta. Add the Parmesan and continue to cook over a low heat for about 5 minutes, until the polenta thickens.

SAUCES

ONION GRAVY

Serves 4

3 tbsp ***OLIVE OIL***
3 ***RED ONIONS****, peeled and finely sliced*
5 tbsp ***BALSAMIC VINEGAR***
½ cup ***MADEIRA*** *or brandy (optional)*
1 ***BEEF STOCK*** *cube*
1 tsp ***CORNFLOUR***
1 cup (250ml) ***WATER****, warm*
25g ***BUTTER***
2 tsp ***WORCESTERSHIRE SAUCE***
SALT *and freshly* ***GROUND BLACK PEPPER***

In a large frying pan heat the oil over a high heat.

Add the sliced onions, reduce the heat to low and fry the onions slowly. Cover the pan and cook for approximately 15 minutes or until the onions are soft.

Remove the lid. Turn the heat back up to high and stir continuously. Pour in the vinegar and Madeira and cook for a further minute to deglaze (see pg 209) the pan.

Melt the beef stock cube and the cornflour in the warm water. Add to the onions with the butter and Worcestershire sauce.

Bring the sauce to the boil and reduce to a simmer until the gravy thickens. Season with salt and pepper to taste.

MUSHROOM SAUCE

Serves 4 (makes 2 cups)

3 tbsp ***OLIVE OIL***
½ ***LEEK****, cleaned, small rough chopped*
4 cloves ***GARLIC****, finely sliced*
300g ***BUTTON MUSHROOMS****, sliced*
1 cup (250ml) ***CREAM***
½ cup ***CHICKEN STOCK*** *or ½ cup water and 1 whole chicken stock cube*
SALT *and freshly* ***GROUND BLACK PEPPER***

In a frying pan over a medium heat, cook the leek and garlic in the oil for 5 minutes. Stir in the mushrooms and cook for a further 5 minutes. Pour in the cream and stock and let the liquid reduce for a few minutes. Taste and season with salt and pepper.

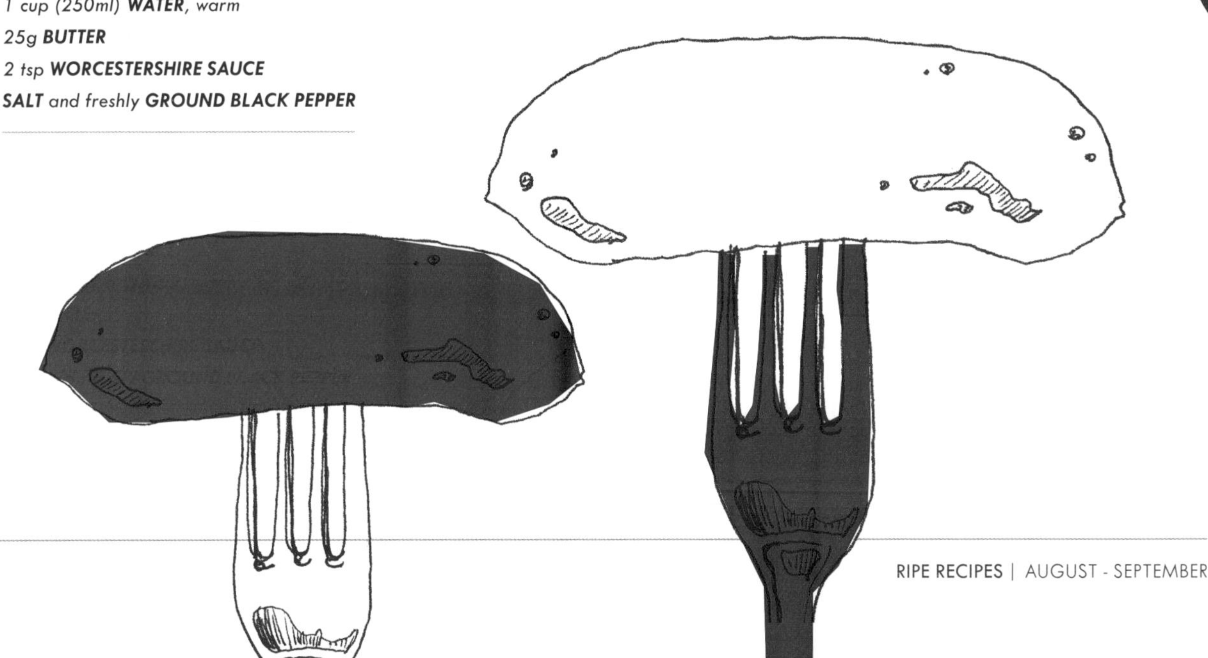

THE GREEN ROOM

CABBAGE & CARAWAY

Serves 6

100g ***BUTTER***
2 tbsp ***VEGETABLE OIL***
1 tsp ***CARAWAY SEEDS***
½ ***SAVOY CABBAGE****, finely sliced*
½ cup (125ml) boiling ***WATER***
SALT *and freshly* ***GROUND BLACK PEPPER***

In a large frying pan over a high heat melt the butter and oil – be careful not to brown the butter. Add the caraway seeds. Stir for 10-15 seconds.

Add the cabbage and boiling water.

Cook for approximately 4 minutes, depending on how crunchy you would like the cabbage, stirring occasionally. Season with salt and lots of freshly ground black pepper. Strain off any excess liquid before serving.

BRUSSELS & BACON

Serves 4-6

500g ***BRUSSELS SPROUTS****, outer leaves removed, stalks trimmed, cut in half lengthways*
2 tbsp ***OLIVE OIL***
100g ***STREAKY BACON****, finely chopped*
ZEST *of 1* ***LEMON***
SALT *and freshly* ***GROUND BLACK PEPPER***

In a large saucepan, bring some salted water to the boil. Add the brussels and cook for 4-5 minutes. Drain and refresh under cold running water, then set aside.

In a large frying pan over a high heat, fry the bacon in the olive oil until crispy. Add the brussels, lemon zest, salt and pepper. Stir to combine.

Heat through for a minute and serve.

PEA MINT PURÉE

Serves 4-6

500g frozen ***GREEN PEAS***
½ cup ***FRESH MINT LEAVES***
30g ***BUTTER***
2 tbsp ***CREAM***
¼ tsp ***SALT***
¼ tsp freshly ***GROUND BLACK PEPPER***

Cook the peas in a saucepan of boiling water for 3-4 minutes.

Drain off the water and return the peas to the saucepan. Add the mint, butter, cream, salt and pepper.

Purée with a stick blender or in a food processor and serve.

CREAMED SILVERBEET WITH HORSERADISH

Serves 6-8

600g ***SILVERBEET****, stems and leaves separated*
1 cup (250ml) ***WATER***
½ cup (125ml) ***VEGETABLE STOCK***
3 tbsp ***CREAMED HORSERADISH***
1 cup (250ml) ***CREAM***
½ cup (120g) ***SOUR CREAM***
SALT *and freshly* ***GROUND BLACK PEPPER***

Finely dice the silverbeet stems and coarsely chop the leaves.

Place the water and stock in a large frying pan. When simmering add the silverbeet and cook for approximately 5 minutes or until soft and wilted.

Most of the liquid should have evaporated, but if not drain it off. Add the horseradish, cream and sour cream. Heat for a minute to warm through.

Remove from the heat and pulse with a stick blender until roughly smooth but not puréed.

Season with salt and pepper to taste.

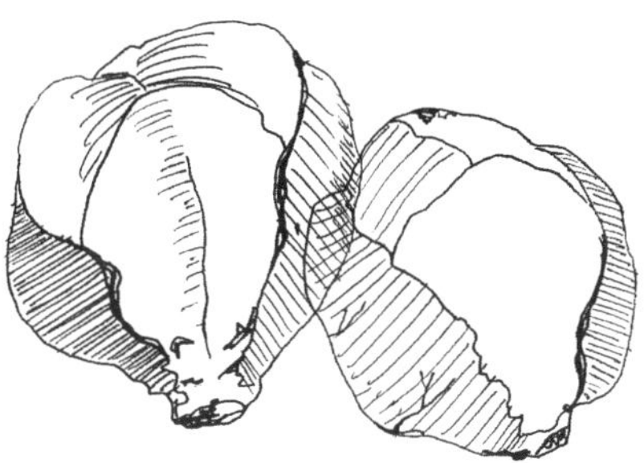

"I eat my peas with honey. I've done it all my life. It makes the peas taste funny but it keeps them on the knife." – Anon as quoted by Foster Redfern

CHOCOLATE & NUT KISSES

You can substitute walnuts and dates with cranberries and brazil nuts for a different flavour.

Makes approx 10 sandwich biscuits

*85g **UNSALTED BUTTER**, softened*
*½ cup (80g) soft **BROWN SUGAR***
*1 cup (150g) plain **FLOUR***
*1 tsp **BAKING POWDER***
*1 tbsp **COCOA***
*1 tbsp **MILK***
*½ cup (75g) **WALNUTS**, roughly chopped*
*1 cup (150g) **DATES**, finely chopped*
*½ of the **CHOCOLATE BUTTERCREAM ICING** recipe (see pg 134)*

Preheat oven to 180°C.

Line a baking tray with baking paper.

In a bowl, cream the butter and sugar until light and fluffy. Sift the dry ingredients together and add alternately with the milk to the creamed butter and sugar.

Add walnuts and dates and fold to combine.

Roll the mixture into walnut sized balls, approximately 25g of uncooked dough. Lay on the lined tray. Press each biscuit with a fork to flatten slightly and bake for 15 minutes.

Allow to cool before sandwiching together with chocolate buttercream icing (see pg 134).

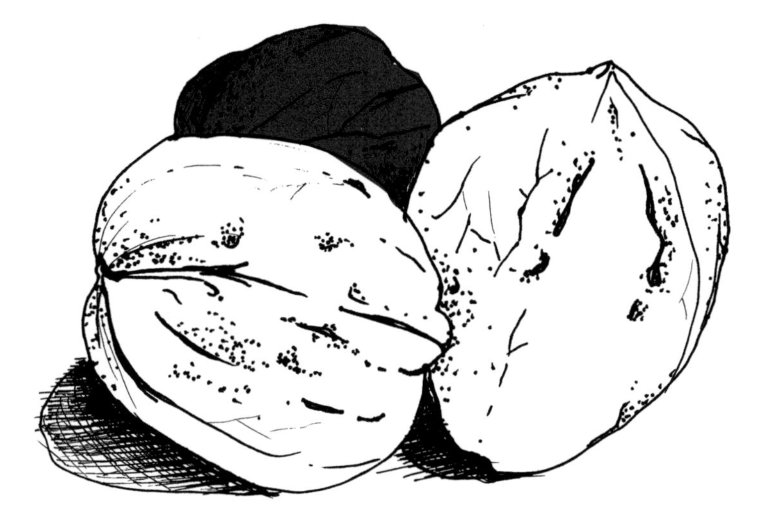

"That's the way the cookie crumbles." – Anon

ORANGE & ALMOND CAKE

This cake is a winner with friends and loved ones who are wheat and dairy intolerant. It keeps well and is great served with a dollop of crème fraiche.

Serves 8-10

3 whole ***ORANGES****, scrubbed clean with skin on, topped and tailed*
1 whole ***LEMON****, scrubbed clean with skin on, topped and tailed*
9 large ***EGGS***
1 cup (220g) ***CASTER SUGAR***
4 cups (400g) ***GROUND ALMONDS***
1 tsp ***BAKING POWDER***
1 tsp ***VANILLA EXTRACT****, or 1 vanilla pod*
½ cup (60g) sliced ***ALMONDS***

CITRUS SYRUP

1 cup (250ml) ***LEMON JUICE***
1 cup (220g) ***CASTER SUGAR***

Preheat oven to 180°C.

Grease and line with baking paper a 26cm spring form tin with baking paper.

In a medium sized saucepan arrange the oranges and lemon so that they fit snugly. Fill with water to a level two-thirds of the way up the side of the fruit. Place over a medium heat and bring to the boil.

Keep an eye on it. After approximately 10 minutes of boiling turn the lemon and oranges over. Continue cooking until the fruit has softened and the water has nearly evaporated.

Remove the saucepan from the heat and cut all the fruit into chunky pieces, removing any visible pips. Place the pieces into a food processor and purée while still hot.

Add the eggs, sugar, almonds, baking powder and vanilla to the puréed fruit and process for a minute until thick and smooth.

Pour into the lined tin, sprinkle with the sliced almonds and bake for 30 to 40 minutes. Test by pushing a skewer into the centre. When removed a wet crumbly mixture should remain on the skewer.

To prepare the citrus syrup: in a small saucepan over a medium to high heat combine the caster sugar and juice. Bring to the boil, dissolving the sugar. Continue boiling to let the liquid reduce until syrupy in consistency.

With a skewer, pierce holes into the cake to allow the syrup to sink in. Pour half the syrup over the cake while still hot. Remove from the tin and serve with the remaining syrup.

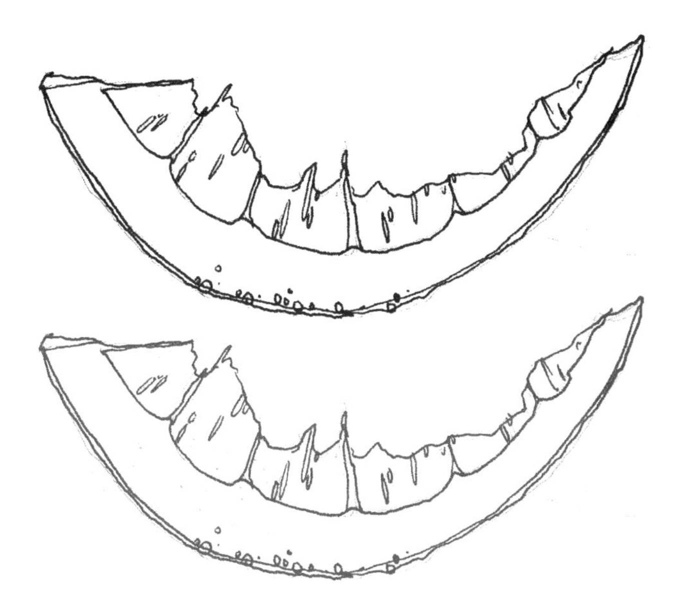

"What my mother believed about cooking is that if you worked hard enough and prospered, someone else would do it for you." – Anon

PUMPKIN PIES

Makes enough filling for 24 muffin tin sized tart shells or 1 large 26cm fluted tart tin

1½ cups ***CROWN PUMPKIN****, cooked and mashed*
1 tsp ***GROUND CINNAMON***
½ tsp ***GROUND GINGER***
½ tsp ***GROUND NUTMEG***
¼ tsp ***GROUND CLOVES***
2 ***EGGS***
1 cup (250ml) ***MILK***
½ tsp ***SALT***
1 cup (220g) ***CASTER SUGAR***
¼ cup (90g) ***MAPLE SYRUP*** *(optional)*

Preheat oven to 180°C.

Line your tin of choice with uncooked sweet pastry and keep chilled.

Combine all the ground spices with the mashed pumpkin.

In a mixing bowl beat together the eggs, milk, salt and sugar. Add this to the pumpkin mixture, combining until smooth.

Pour into uncooked mini tart shells and cook for approximately 30 minutes or until set.

When using a 26cm tart tin bake for 45 minutes or until set.

Drizzle with maple syrup while still warm.

SWEET PASTRY FOR TARTS

330g plain ***FLOUR***
180g ***UNSALTED BUTTER****, cold cut into small cubes*
100g ***ICING SUGAR***
ZEST *of 1* ***ORANGE***
¼ tsp ***SALT***
1 EGG YOLK
2-4 tbsp cold ***WATER***

Place the flour, butter, icing sugar, zest and salt into the bowl of a food processor. Pulse together until you achieve a coarse bread crumb consistency. Add the egg yolk and water. Pulse until the dough begins to come together. You may need to add a little bit of extra water.

Remove from the bowl and shape into a smooth disc. Wrap the disc in cling film and chill in the fridge or freezer until ready to use.

When you're ready to roll the pastry, remove it from the fridge and leave for 5-10 minutes, just to take the chill off. If using ready made pastry sheets remove from freezer to defrost.

Grease your tin of choice.

Roll the pastry until it measures about 5mm thick and line your tin, or using a ring cutter cut out rounds to fit the muffin tins.

RIPE BREAD & BUTTER PUDDINGS

Serves 4-6

4-6 ***CROISSANTS*** *or danish pastries*
1 cup frozen ***BERRIES***
½ cup (100g) ***CHOCOLATE BUTTONS****, optional*
1 ***BANANA****, sliced*
4 ***EGGS****, beaten*
400ml ***CREAM***
2 tsp ***VANILLA EXTRACT***
¼ cup (40g) soft ***BROWN SUGAR***
1 tsp ***GROUND CINNAMON***
2 tbsp ***DEMERARA SUGAR*** *or raw sugar*

Preheat oven to 180°C.

Grease and line a 20cm cake tin for a single pudding or make individual desserts in a 6 hole large Texas sized muffin pan. Line with cupcake cases.

Cut the croissants roughly into 2cm pieces. Place in a bowl with the berries, chocolate buttons and banana. In a separate bowl mix together the eggs, cream, vanilla and brown sugar until combined. Pour over the croissant mixture and stir well.

Fill the tin or tins with the mixture, which should be quite wet. Sprinkle with the cinnamon and sugar.

Bake in the oven for 30-35 minutes. Best served warm with custard or ice cream.

LEMON HONEY

This is always such a useful thing to have in your fridge. Try to use it in some of these ways:

Split a lemon sour cream cake and fill with curd and cream, make lemon poppy seed muffins and add a dollop to the centre before baking, make tiny lemon tarts by blind baking mini pastry cases and filling with lemon curd, sandwich together melting moment biscuits with curd or just slather it on your toast or gingerbread.

Makes approximately 500ml

JUICE** and **ZEST** of 6 **LEMONS
*185g **UNSALTED BUTTER***
*3 cups (660g) **CASTER SUGAR***
*6 **EGGS**, lightly beaten*

Grate only the yellow skin off the lemons, avoiding the bitter white pith. Juice the lemons and strain into a bowl, removing the pips.

In a large saucepan gently melt the butter. Add the lemon juice, zest and sugar and stir with a wooden spoon over a medium heat until the sugar is dissolved.

Lower the heat slightly. Add the eggs to the saucepan and stir quickly so as not to cook them. Be careful not to catch the curd on the bottom of the pan. Keep stirring for 10-15 minutes or until the mixture has thickened.

Dip a wooden spoon into the mixture and tap off the excess. Run your finger along the back of the spoon – if the line holds, the curd is ready.

Push the curd through a sieve into a large bowl. While still hot pour into sterilised jars and seal (see pg 209). Allow to cool and keep stored in the fridge.

PRESERVED LEMONS OR LIMES

A great addition to your fridge to keep on hand and a great gift for people too.

Approx 4-6 jars

*8 **LEMONS** or 12-16 limes*
*250g **COARSE SEA SALT***
*1ltr **WATER***
*4-6 **RED** or **GREEN CHILLIES***
*4-6 **BAY LEAVES***

In a large saucepan, bring some water to the boil, enough to cover the lemons or limes. Add the fruit and boil for 5 minutes. Drain and rinse the fruit in cold water.

Trim the ends of the lemons and cut into quarters or large wedges. Using half the salt spread it over the flesh of the lemons. In another saucepan bring the litre of water and rest of the salt to a boil. Remove from heat.

Pack the cut fruit into sterilised jars, packing down to make a firm fit.

Add a chilli and a bay leaf to each jar. Fill each jar with the hot salt water brine. Seal the jar. Keep in cool storage or refrigerator for 4-6 weeks before using.

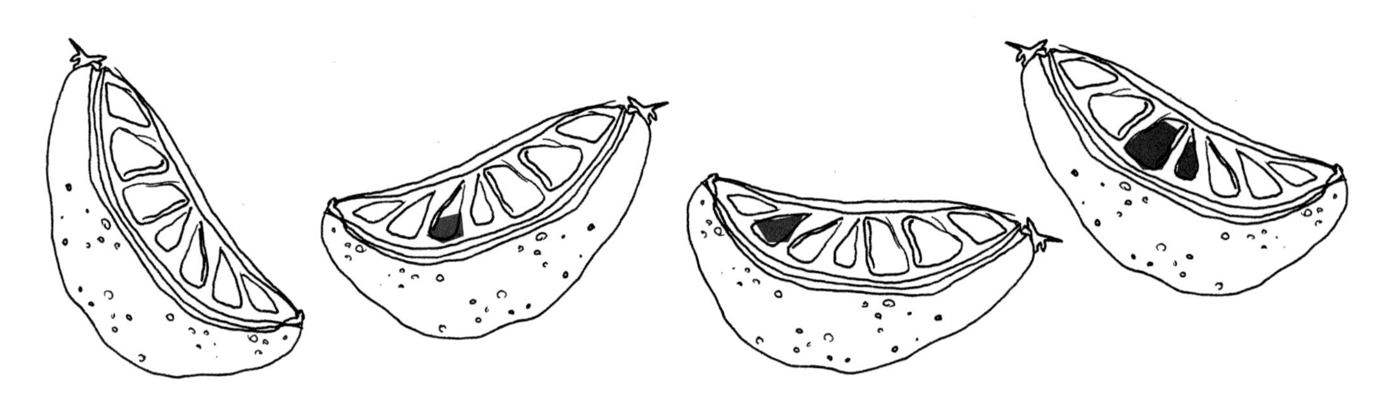

Asparagus. Parsnips. New season potatoes. Swedes. Carrots. Lettuces. Broad beans. Globe artichokes. Silverbeet. Beetroot. Peas. Parsley. Mint. Florence fennel. Rocket. Rhubarb. Kumara.

OCTOBER | NOVEMBER

One word – Asparagus!

SMOOTHIES

You can really experiment with these smoothies. They are easy recipes to adjust to dairy free options with juice, soy, rice, or coconut milk alternatives.

Thank you Katie Wallace (our "Smoothie Queen") for coming to the "shake" party with these recipes!

Each recipe serves 2

SOY BREAKFAST

*1 **BANANA**, peeled and chopped*
*1⅓ cups (340ml) of your favourite **SOY MILK***
*1 tsp **LIQUID HONEY***
*2 tbsp **LSA** (ground linseed, sunflower seeds and almonds)*
*¼ tsp **VANILLA EXTRACT***
*2 tsp **WHEAT GERM***
*½ cup crushed **ICE** (optional) or ½ cup soy ice cream*

Place all ingredients into a blender and whizz.

Serve with a little fresh nutmeg grated on top.

YOGHURT BERRY

*1 cup frozen **BERRIES**, any kind is great*
*½ cup crushed **ICE** (optional)*
*½ cup **VANILLA ICE CREAM***
*2 tbsp **LIQUID HONEY***
*1 cup (250ml) **MILK***
*½ **BANANA**, peeled and chopped*
*4 tbsp **NATURAL UNSWEETENED YOGHURT***

Place all ingredients into a blender and whizz.

DAIRY FREE BERRY

*1 **APPLE**, cored and chopped*
*½ cup crushed **ICE***
*1 cup frozen **BERRIES***
*1 tsp **LIQUID HONEY***
*350ml **APPLE** juice*

Place all ingredients into a blender and whizz.

DATE, BANANA & ALMOND

*1 handful of blanched **ALMONDS***
*½ cup crushed **ICE***
*1 **BANANA**, peeled and chopped*
*350ml **MILK** (soy milk or rice milk also goes really well)*
*10 **DATES**, pitted and roughly chopped*

Blitz the almonds quickly first to achieve a roughly chopped effect. Add the remaining ingredients to the blender and whizz.

Roman Dunbar

BRIOCHE

The original and best brioche on Richmond Road. . . our locals love them.

Amy Wong Kam brought brioche onto the scene at Ripe. She's a purist at heart and feels that you can't beat the delicate flavour of the yeasty dough with the cinnamon sugar warm out of the oven, accompanied by a fresh coffee. We agree!

Brioche dough is best left loosely covered overnight in the fridge to prove and double in size.

MAKES 12 large – using a Texas-sized muffin tin (1 cup capacity) or 24 medium – using a standard cupcake tin (½ cup capacity)

500ml ***MILK****, tepid*
1 tbsp ***DRIED YEAST***
4 large ***EGGS***
½ cup (110g) ***CASTER SUGAR***
250g ***UNSALTED BUTTER****, melted*
½ tbsp ***SALT***
850g ***BAKERS FLOUR*** *or a similar strong white flour*

In a medium sized bowl pour in the tepid milk and sprinkle over the dried yeast.

Cover and set aside in a warm place for a few minutes for the yeast to activate. It will begin to bubble up.

In a large bowl whisk together the eggs, sugar, melted butter and salt until the sugar has dissolved and the eggs are getting frothy.

Add the yeast mixture to the eggs and stir to combine.

Add the flour to the middle of this mix. With a metal spoon, stir vigorously for 5 to 10 minutes until the dough becomes glossy.

The mixture will be wet. If it looks too wet add a little more flour, just a tablespoon at a time.

If you plan to use the brioche dough on the same day, place the bowl in a warm place and cover loosely. Allow to double in size.

Otherwise, prove it overnight by covering it with cling film and keeping it in the fridge.

CINNAMON BRIOCHE

VEGETABLE OIL *for greasing*
1 cup (160g) soft ***BROWN SUGAR***
3 tsp ***GROUND CINNAMON***
250g ***UNSALTED BUTTER****, cold*

Preheat oven to 180°C.

Brush the tins lightly with oil to coat.

Empty the dough from the bowl onto a floured bench. Press the dough lightly into a rectangle with a 2-3cm thickness – the dough will be very soft. Sprinkle over the brown sugar and cinnamon in quantities to suit your taste. Grate the cold butter over the sugar.

Roll from the longest side to form a log. Slice the log into 3-4cm thick slices. Place the dough into the tins. Leave the tins in a warm place to prove the dough. Check after 20 minutes by giving the dough a gentle poke with your finger to see if it's "puffy".

Bake in hot oven for 15-20 minutes or until golden brown.

Remove from the oven. Take the brioche out of trays while still hot to avoid the sugar sticking to the tray. Be careful of the hot sugar.

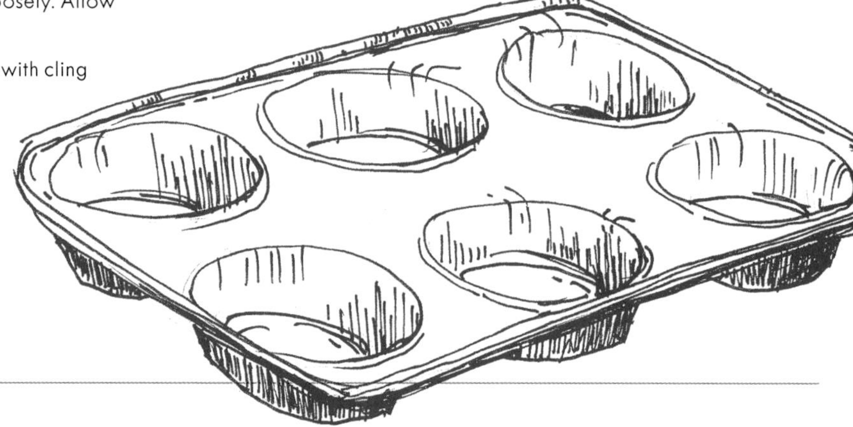

FILLED BRIOCHE

Try some of these ideas:

1 cup ***LEMON CURD***

1 cup frozen ***BERRIES*** *and*
1 cup ***WHITE CHOCOLATE CHIPS***

3 ***PEARS****, peeled, cored and chopped and*
1 cup ***DARK CHOCOLATE CHIPS***

½ cup ***STEWED FRUIT*** *and*
½ cup of ***VANILLA CUSTARD***

7-8 fresh ***PLUMS****, stones removed and cut into wedges and*
¼ cup ***CREAM CHEESE***

Preheat oven to 180°C.

Lightly brush the tins with oil.

Gently pat the dough out onto a floured bench into a large rectangle.

Cut the dough into 6-7cm square pieces. Place the squares into muffin tins with the corners overhanging.

Put 2 teaspoons of the sweet filling of your choice in the centre. Pick up the corners of the square and fold gently over to meet in the centre. Press lightly and sprinkle with brown sugar.

Prove in a warm place for approximately 15 minutes or until the dough looks puffy.

Bake in a hot oven for 15-20 minutes or until golden.

ASPARAGUS TART

Just as good without the ham for a vegetarian option. If you are not a fan of mustard, pesto is a great alternative.

*2 sheets (500g) frozen **FLAKY PUFF PASTRY***
*4 tsp **WHOLEGRAIN MUSTARD***
*¾ cup (90g) **TASTY CHEESE**, grated*
*100g **HAM**, sliced*
*10 fresh **ASPARAGUS** spears, trim any woody ends*
*½ cup (40g) **PARMESAN**, grated*
SALT** and freshly **GROUND BLACK PEPPER

Preheat oven to 200°C.

Line an oven tray with baking paper. Place one sheet of puff pastry down on it. Spread it with 2 teaspoons of the wholegrain mustard.

Sprinkle ¼ cup of the grated cheese over the base layer of pastry.

Lay the next pastry layer on top, lining up the edges. Spread with the remaining mustard, keeping a 1cm edge border of plain pastry. Lay on the ham and asparagus. Sprinkle with the remaining cheese and Parmesan.

Season with salt and freshly ground black pepper.

Score criss-crosses around the pastry border with a sharp knife.

Bake the tart in a hot oven for 30-35 minutes. Lift the pastry base to ensure it is cooked golden underneath.

BREAKFAST BURRITOS

Serves 4

OLIVE OIL
*4 **FIELD MUSHROOMS**, brushed clean and kept whole*
*2 **TOMATOES**, halved*
*8 rashers **STREAKY** free range **BACON***
*2 **CHORIZO SAUSAGES**, sliced lengthways*
*4 knobs of **BUTTER***
*1 tbsp **FRESH THYME LEAVES***
*6 **EGGS***
*¼ cup (60ml) **CREAM***
*4 large **TORTILLAS** (25cm diameter works well)*
***HP** sauce or spicy tomato relish (see pg 82)*
*1 large handful of **FRESH BABY SPINACH LEAVES***
*4 slices of **TASTY CHEESE***
SALT** and freshly **GROUND BLACK PEPPER
*Your favourite **MAYONNAISE***

Preheat oven to 200°C.

Lightly oil an oven tray. Arrange the mushrooms, tomatoes, bacon and chorizo on the tray. Place a small knob of butter on each mushroom and sprinkle the thyme over the tomatoes. Roast in the oven for 15 minutes.

To prepare the scrambled the eggs: place them in a bowl with the cream and whisk together. Place a frying pan over a high heat, add a drizzle of oil then pour the egg mixture into the frying pan and scramble. Season with salt and pepper to taste.

To assemble the burritos: lay out tortillas and smear with HP sauce or relish. In the middle of the tortilla place the spinach, egg, tomato, mushroom, bacon and chorizo and cheese. Season with salt and pepper.

Drizzle with a little mayonnaise. Fold the bottom side up to meet in the middle then tuck the sides in, resulting in an open ended rectangle a little like an envelope. Fold the last side in and toast in the oven for 10 minutes or grill in a sandwich press to seal.

"All happiness depends on a leisurely breakfast" – John Ginther.

ROASTED PORK BELLY WITH ASIAN GREENS

If you are lucky enough to have any leftover pork belly, try it in a fresh ciabatta bap with apple sauce. Alternatively, chop it up and toss through the Rice Noodle Salad *(see pg 184).*

Serves 6

1-1.5kg **PORK BELLY**, bone out, skin intact and heavily scored with a knife
Drizzle of **OLIVE OIL**
2 tsp **SALT**
3 cloves **GARLIC**, finely chopped
2 tbsp **SOY SAUCE**
1 tbsp **OLIVE OIL**
1 tsp **SESAME OIL**
1 tsp **CHINESE 5 SPICE**
2 tbsp **SPICY PLUM SAUCE** (see pg 83)
2 **CARROTS**, roughly diced
2 **ONIONS**, peeled, roughly diced
2 stalks **CELERY**, roughly diced
6 whole **STAR ANISE**
1 **BAY LEAF**, ripped
3 cups (750ml) **WATER**

Preheat oven to 160°C.

Rub the olive oil and salt into the scored skin of the pork.

In a small bowl mix together the garlic, soy sauce, olive oil, sesame oil, Chinese 5 Spice and plum sauce. Rub this onto the belly of pork, not the skin.

In a large, deep sided roasting pan place the carrots, onions, celery, star anise, bay leaf and water. Rest the pork on top of the vegetables and water. Cover the whole roasting pan with tin foil and cook for 2½ hours.

Increase the oven temperature to 250°C.

Remove the tin foil and cook for a further 30 minutes. If the skin is not crispy enough after the full 3 hours, switch the oven to grill and position the pork belly in the middle of the oven. It should crackle up quickly but keep an eye on it so that it doesn't burn.

Rest the meat. Prepare the Asian greens.

ASIAN GREENS

6 **BOK CHOY**, washed and quartered
1 bunch **BROCCOLINI**
2 tbsp **SESAME OIL**
2 tbsp **VEGETABLE OIL**
2 cloves **GARLIC**, finely sliced
2 **SPRING ONIONS**, chopped into 2cm lengths
½ cup (125ml) **OYSTER SAUCE**
2 tbsp **SOY SAUCE**
JUICE of ½ **LEMON**

Bring a saucepan of water to the boil, blanch the green vegetables for 1-2 minutes and refresh in iced cold water. Drain and pat dry with a clean cloth.

In a small saucepan heat both the oils over a medium heat. Add the garlic and spring onion and cook for 3 minutes. Pour in the oyster, soy and lemon juice and stir to combine. Heat for another few minutes then pour the sauce over the blanched vegetables. Top with thick slices of the tender pork belly.

CHICKEN MARBELLA

This is a slight variation on the classic dish first created in THE SILVER PALATE COOKBOOK. The combination of sweet, salty and sour is wonderful. Delicious served with a mash from the S&M pages (see pg 160).

Serves 4-6

4-6 whole **CHICKEN LEGS**, drumstick and thigh, bone in and skin on
6 cloves **GARLIC**, peeled and crushed
1 tbsp **DRIED OREGANO**
SALT and freshly **GROUND BLACK PEPPER**
½ cup (125ml) **RED WINE VINEGAR**
12 (100g) whole pitted **PRUNES**, soaked in boiling water to plump up
¼ cup (40g) **CAPERS**
16 large **GREEN SPANISH OLIVES** or 1 cup mixed olives
2 **BAY LEAVES**, torn
½ cup (80g) soft **BROWN SUGAR**
1 cup (250ml) **WHITE WINE**
¼ cup **FRESH ITALIAN PARSLEY**, finely chopped

Preheat oven to 170°C.

In a large bowl combine the chicken, garlic, oregano, salt, pepper, vinegar, prunes, capers, olives and bay leaves. Leave to marinate in the fridge for at least 2-3 hours.

In a large, deep ovenproof dish arrange the chicken in a single layer. Spoon the marinade over evenly. Sprinkle with brown sugar. Pour the white wine around the chicken.

Bake for approximately 1¼ hours. Remove from oven, skim off any excess oil. Sprinkle with chopped parsley.

RICE NOODLE SALAD

Serve this salad with the Roasted Pork Belly with Asian Greens (see pg 182). Alternatively, for another meal idea toss through stir fried chicken, beef or pork.

Serves 4-6

200g **DRIED RICE NOODLES**
a dash of **VEGETABLE OIL**
200g **GREEN BEANS**, trimmed and sliced on an angle
2 whole **BOK CHOY**, quartered
1 bunch **BROCCOLINI**, stem trimmed
¼ **RED ONION**, peeled and finely sliced lengthways
1 cup (80g) fresh **MUNG BEAN SPROUTS**
1 cup **FRESH CORIANDER LEAVES**, stalks and leaves finely sliced

DRESSING

1 tbsp **SESAME OIL**
2 tsp **SESAME SEEDS**, toasted (see pg 211)
1 fresh **RED CHILLI**, seeds removed, finely sliced
4 cloves **GARLIC**, peeled and crushed
JUICE and **ZEST** of 2 **LEMONS**
2 tbsp **FISH SAUCE**
2 tbsp **DARK SOY SAUCE**
1 tsp soft **BROWN SUGAR**
2 tbsp **SWEET CHILLI SAUCE**

Bring a large saucepan of water to the boil. Add the dried noodles and cook until soft, approximately 3 minutes. Drain and refresh in cold water and drain again. Toss with a little oil. Set aside.

Bring another large saucepan of water to the boil. Blanch the beans, bok choy and broccolini for 1-2 minutes. Remove and refresh in iced cold water. Drain well.

To prepare the dressing: place all the dressing ingredients in a jar with a tight fitting lid. Shake together until the sugar has dissolved.

To assemble: place the rice noodles in a large serving bowl. Pour half of the dressing over the noodles and toss to coat.

Add the red onion, bean sprouts, coriander, bok choy, green beans and broccolini and stir to combine. Pour over the remainder of the dressing and serve.

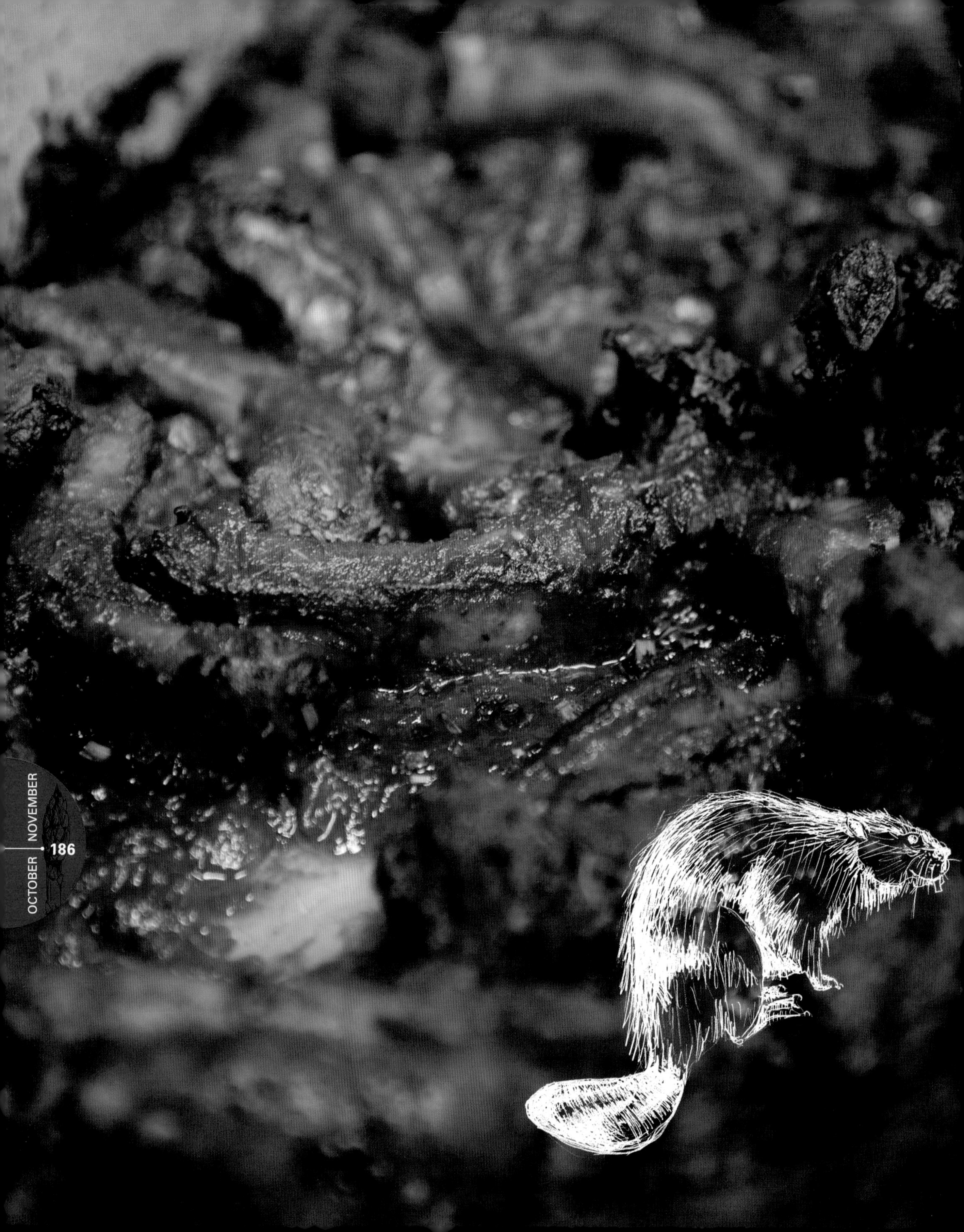

BEAVER'S "LET THEM PIG OUT" RIBS

A good friend of mine, Nicole Beaver, let us have this sticky rib recipe. They are best served with jacket potatoes and a fresh salad from the Slaw Floor *(see pg 192)**. Delicious!*

This is a sweet, Southern style bbq sauce that goes all sticky. Ask your butcher to single cut the rack of ribs for you.

The sauce can be made a few days before it is needed – simply store in the fridge.

Serves 6

BBQ SAUCE

1 tbsp ***OIL***
1 ***ONION****, peeled, finely chopped*
4 cloves ***GARLIC****, finely chopped*
2 cups (500ml) ***TOMATO SAUCE***
1 cup (250ml) ***TOMATO PURÉE***
2 tbsp ***POMEGRANATE MOLASSES*** *(optional)*
½ tsp ***DRIED CHILLI FLAKES***
1 tsp ***SMOKED PAPRIKA***
½ cup (125ml) ***CIDER VINEGAR***
1 cup (160g) soft ***BROWN SUGAR***
¼ cup (60ml) ***WORCESTERSHIRE SAUCE***
2 tbsp ***HONEY***

2kg ***PORK RIBS****, separated*

To prepare the BBQ sauce: heat the oil in a frying pan over a medium heat. Cook the onions and garlic until they are soft and translucent, approximately 10 minutes. Add all the remaining ingredients and simmer gently for 30 minutes.

Leave the sauce to cool, then store in the fridge until ready to use.

To marinate the ribs: in a large bowl mix half of the sauce in with the pork ribs. Leave in the fridge for a few hours or overnight. The longer the better.

Preheat oven to 140°C.

To cook the ribs: in a large deep sided roasting pan, spread out the ribs. Pour over the remaining bbq sauce evenly. Cover the pan with tin foil. Roast the ribs for approximately 2 hours. Turn and baste occasionally.

Increase the oven temperature to 200°C. Remove the foil and cook for a further 20 minutes turning occasionally.

It is important at this stage to keep an eye on the ribs so they do not burn.

By now they will be sticky, delicious and ready to devour.

Leila Hannah

Helava Tekela-Pule

PUMPKIN SAGE RISOTTO WITH CRISPY PANCETTA

When cooking risotto make sure you have the stock warm and everything you need ready to go as the cooking method will consume your time.

Serves 6

6-7 cups (1.5ltr) ***CHICKEN STOCK***
2 tbsp ***OLIVE OIL***
50g ***BUTTER***
2 medium ***RED ONIONS****, peeled, finely diced*
4 stalks of ***CELERY****, finely diced*
8 cloves ***GARLIC****, finely chopped*
ZEST *of 1* ***LEMON***
½ cup ***FRESH SAGE****, chopped*
500g ***PUMPKIN****, peeled and diced into 1cm cubes*
2 cups (400g) ***ARBORIO RICE***
1 cup (250ml) ***WHITE WINE***
1 cup (80g) ***PARMESAN****, grated (reserve half for serving)*
SALT *and freshly* ***GROUND BLACK PEPPER***
knob of ***BUTTER***
½ cup ***FRESH SAGE****, whole leaves*
100g ***PANCETTA****, slices ripped into small pieces*

Place a large saucepan on a medium to high heat. Add stock and bring to the boil. Reduce the heat to a gentle simmer.

Place a heavy based large saucepan over a medium heat. Add the olive oil and butter. When hot add the onion, celery, garlic and lemon zest. Cook for few minutes or until the onion is soft.

Add the chopped sage and pumpkin and cook for a further 2 minutes. Add your rice and cook stirring constantly for approximately 3 minutes or until the grains have become slightly translucent.

Pour in the wine and allow it to reduce for a minute or two. Start adding your stock one ladle at a time. Each time allow the liquid to be absorbed almost entirely. Remember to keep stirring.

When you have added approximately 5 cups of the stock (one ladle at a time) the pumpkin should be cooked but still holding its shape and the rice al dente (firm in texture but not hard). If not, add one more cup of stock and cook for a bit longer. This should take 20-25 minutes.

When the rice is cooked to your liking, remove from the heat. Add half of the Parmesan and stir to combine. Season well with salt and pepper and allow to rest for 5 minutes before serving. If you like a slightly wet risotto add one more cup of the hot stock.

Place a frying pan over a medium heat and melt the knob of butter. Fry the whole sage leaves for 1 minute. Add the pancetta and continue cooking until the pancetta and the sage are crispy.

Into individual serving bowls place the risotto. Sprinkle over remaining Parmesan, a few of the whole sage leaves and some pancetta.

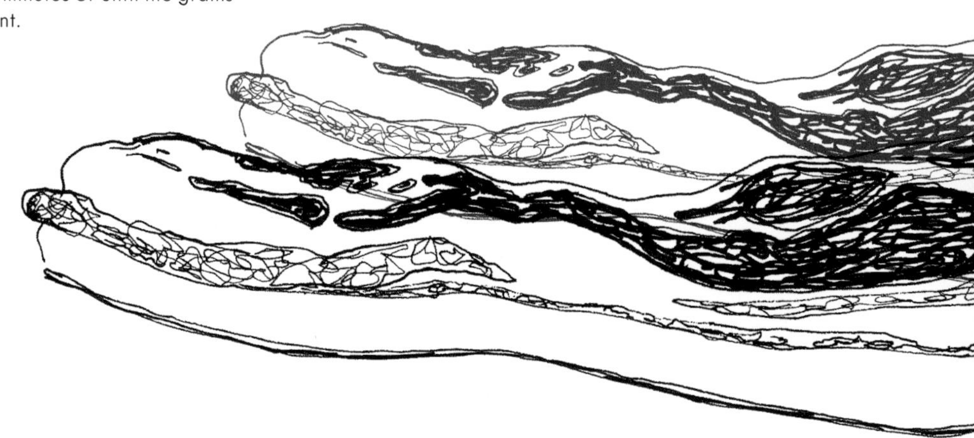

BUCKWHEAT & BROAD BEAN SALAD

Serves 6-8

½ cup (100g) **BUCKWHEAT**
500g **BROAD BEANS**, *fresh or frozen*
¼ **GREEN CABBAGE**, *finely sliced*
2 large raw **COURGETTES**, *coarsely grated*
1 cup **FRESH MINT LEAVES**, *torn*
5 **ARTICHOKE HEARTS**, *drained and sliced*
250g **COTTAGE CHEESE**

DRESSING

JUICE of 2-3 **LEMONS**, **ZEST** of 1
½ cup (125ml) **OLIVE OIL**
½ cup (125ml) **WHITE WINE VINEGAR**
2 tbsp **HONEY**
SALT and freshly **GROUND BLACK PEPPER**

Cook the buckwheat (see pg 210).

To prepare the dressing: place all the dressing ingredients in a jar with a tight fitting lid and shake well.

To prepare the salad: blanch broad beans for 2-3 minutes in a large saucepan of boiling water. Drain and refresh in iced cold water. Drain. Remove and discard the skins.

In a large bowl combine the cabbage, broad beans, courgette, mint, artichoke and buckwheat.

Add the cottage cheese and the dressing and toss to serve. Taste and season with salt and pepper if needed.

TOFU, MUSHROOM & BROWN RICE SALAD

Serves 4-6

½ cup (100g) **BROWN RICE**
2 **BOK CHOY**, *kept whole with ends trimmed*
1 cup (120g) **EDAMAME BEANS**
VEGETABLE OIL *for frying*
200g firm **TOFU**, *cut into 2cm cubes*
16 **BUTTON MUSHROOMS**, *cut in quarters*
2 **SPRING ONIONS**, *roughly chopped*
1 cup (165g) **UNSALTED PEANUTS**, *roughly chopped, toasted (see pg 211)*
200g **FRESH BEAN SPROUTS**
1 cup **FRESH CORIANDER LEAVES**, *roughly chopped*
1 **CARROT**, *peeled and julienned (thin batons)*
½ cup (60g) **SESAME SEEDS**, *toasted, to garnish (see pg 211)*
SALT and freshly **GROUND BLACK PEPPER**

ASIAN DRESSING

JUICE of ½ a **LEMON**
3 tbsp **SOY SAUCE**
¼ cup (60ml) **SWEET CHILLI SAUCE**
1 tbsp **GINGER**, *freshly grated*
3 tbsp **SESAME OIL**

Cook the brown rice (see pg 211).

To prepare the asian dressing: place all dressing ingredients in a jar with a tight fitting lid and shake well.

To prepare the salad: place a large saucepan of water over a high heat and bring to the boil. Blanch the bok choy and edamame beans for 1 minute, remove and refresh in iced cold water. Drain well. Cut bok choy into quarters lengthways.

Place a frying pan over a medium heat. Pour in a good dash of vegetable oil and fry off the tofu cubes along with the mushrooms. Turn once and cook until golden. Drain on kitchen paper.

In a large bowl, combine the cooked brown rice, spring onions, bok choy, edamame, peanuts, bean sprouts, fresh coriander leaves, carrot, tofu and mushrooms.

Mix the dressing through the salad. Sprinkle with toasted sesame seeds and season with salt and pepper if needed.

THE SLAW FLOOR

We feel coleslaws are underrated. They are cheap to prepare and last well in the fridge. A great all year round salad. Serve as a side with hot ham, steak, ribs, chicken, or use as a sandwich filling.

NUTTY SLAW

Serves 4-6

¼ cup (30g) ***CASHEWS****, roughly chopped*
3 tbsp ***SESAME SEEDS****, toatsed (see pg 211)*
¼ cup (15g) ***LONG THREAD COCONUT***
3 cups ***GREEN CABBAGE****, finely shredded*
3 cups ***RED CABBAGE****, finely shredded*
3 ***SPRING ONIONS****, finely sliced*
1 cup ***FRESH CORIANDER LEAVES****, roughly chopped*
1 cup ***FRESH MINT LEAVES****, roughly chopped*

DRESSING

3 tbsp ***SESAME OIL***
3 tbsp ***PEANUT OIL***
3 tbsp ***RICE WINE VINEGAR***
2 tsp ***LIGHT SOY SAUCE***
⅓ cup (100ml) ***SWEET CHILLI SAUCE***
SALT *and freshly* ***GROUND BLACK PEPPER***

Preheat oven 150°C.

To prepare dressing: place the ingredients in a jar with a tightly fitting lid and shake well.

To prepare slaw: place the cashews in a roasting dish with a dash of oil and roast until golden, approximately 10 minutes. Add the sesame seeds and coconut. Cook for a further 1 minute then remove from the oven and allow to cool.

In a large bowl place the green and red cabbage, spring onions and herbs and toss together to combine.

Pour over the dressing and mix well.

Sprinkle the toasted sesame seeds, coconut and cashews over the top to serve.

"COLE" SLAW

Serves 6-8

1 ***GREEN CABBAGE****, finely shredded*
3 large ***CARROTS****, peeled and grated*
SALT *and freshly* ***GROUND BLACK PEPPER***

DRESSING

¾ cup ***AIOLI*** *(see pg 204)*
3 tbsp ***SOUR CREAM***
2 tbsp ***WHITE VINEGAR***
2 tbsp ***WHITE SUGAR***
2 tsp ***CELERY SALT***
¼ ***RED ONION****, peeled, finely diced*

To prepare the dressing: place all the dressing ingredients in a bowl and whisk together.

To prepare the slaw: in a large bowl, combine the cabbage and carrot. Pour over the dressing and taste for seasoning.

SEEDY SLAW

Serve 4-6

3 cups ***SAVOY CABBAGE****, finely shredded*
3 cups ***WHITE CABBAGE****, finely shredded*
4 ***SPRING ONIONS****, finely sliced*
1 small handful of ***WATERCRESS***
¼ ***RED ONION****, peeled, finely sliced*
4 ***RADISHES****, cut into matchsticks*
¾ cup (90g) ***MIXED SEEDS*** *(try poppy, sesame and sunflower), toasted (see pg 211)*
1 cup ***FRESH MINT LEAVES***

DRESSING

¾ cup **AIOLI** *(see pg 204) or mayonnaise*
3 *tbsp* **SOUR CREAM**
2 *tbsp* **CREAMED HORSERADISH**
2 *tbsp* **WHITE VINEGAR**
2 *tbsp* **WHITE SUGAR**
2 *tsp* **CELERY SALT**

To prepare the dressing: place all the dressing ingredients in a bowl and whisk together.

To prepare the slaw: in a large bowl place the shredded cabbages, spring onion, watercress, red onion and radish. Pour dressing over the slaw and toss well to combine. Sprinkle over the toasted seeds and fresh mint leaves. Taste for seasoning.

PICKLED SLAW

Serves 6-8

90ml **VEGETABLE OIL**
20g **BUTTER**
5 whole **STAR ANISE**
5 **WHOLE CLOVES** *crushed, or 1 tsp ground cloves*
1 small **RED CABBAGE**, *sliced and shredded*
1 **ONION**, *peeled, finely diced*
80ml **WATER**
6 **APPLES**, *peeled, cored and grated*
¼ *cup (60ml)* **RED WINE VINEGAR**
¼ *cup (90g)* **MAPLE SYRUP**
¼ *cup* **CASTER SUGAR**
1 cup **FRESH CHERVIL**, *roughly chopped*
1 **FENNEL BULB**, *finely sliced, optional*
SALT *and freshly* **GROUND BLACK PEPPER**

In a large frying pan, heat the oil and butter over a medium heat. Add the star anise, clove, cabbage and onion. Cook for 5 minutes or until the cabbage has wilted slightly.

Add the water and grated apple. Cover and simmer for 15 minutes. Add vinegar, maple syrup and sugar. Cook for a further 5 minutes.

Just before serving, stir through the chervil and fennel (if using). Taste and season with salt and pepper.

RAW ENERGY

This has to be our most popular salad. There are various versions out there – ours was perfected by Jo Williams.

Jo worked with me at Ripe at the very beginning. I can't thank her enough for all the ideas and recipes she has given us. Jo now owns a very successful business here in Auckland, Madame Jo Jo's Foodstore. Definitely worth a visit if you haven't yet been.

Serves 4-6

500g raw ***BEETROOT****, peeled and grated*
700g ***CARROT****, peeled and grated*
1 cup ***FRESH MINT LEAVES,*** *roughly chopped*
½ cup (80g) ***RAISINS***
¼ cup (30g) ***SUNFLOWER SEEDS****, toasted (see pg 211)*
¼ cup (30g) ***PUMPKIN SEEDS****, toasted*
½ tsp ***SALT***

DRESSING

2 tbsp ***POMEGRANATE MOLASSES***
2 tbsp ***BALSAMIC VINEGAR***
¼ cup (60ml) ***ORANGE JUICE***
¼ cup (60ml) ***OLIVE OIL***
1 tbsp ***HONEY***

To prepare the dressing: place all the dressing ingredients in a jar with a tight fitting lid. Shake well to combine.

To prepare the salad: in a large serving bowl, combine the beetroot, carrot, mint, raisins, seeds and salt and mix.

Pour over the dressing – toss again when ready to serve.

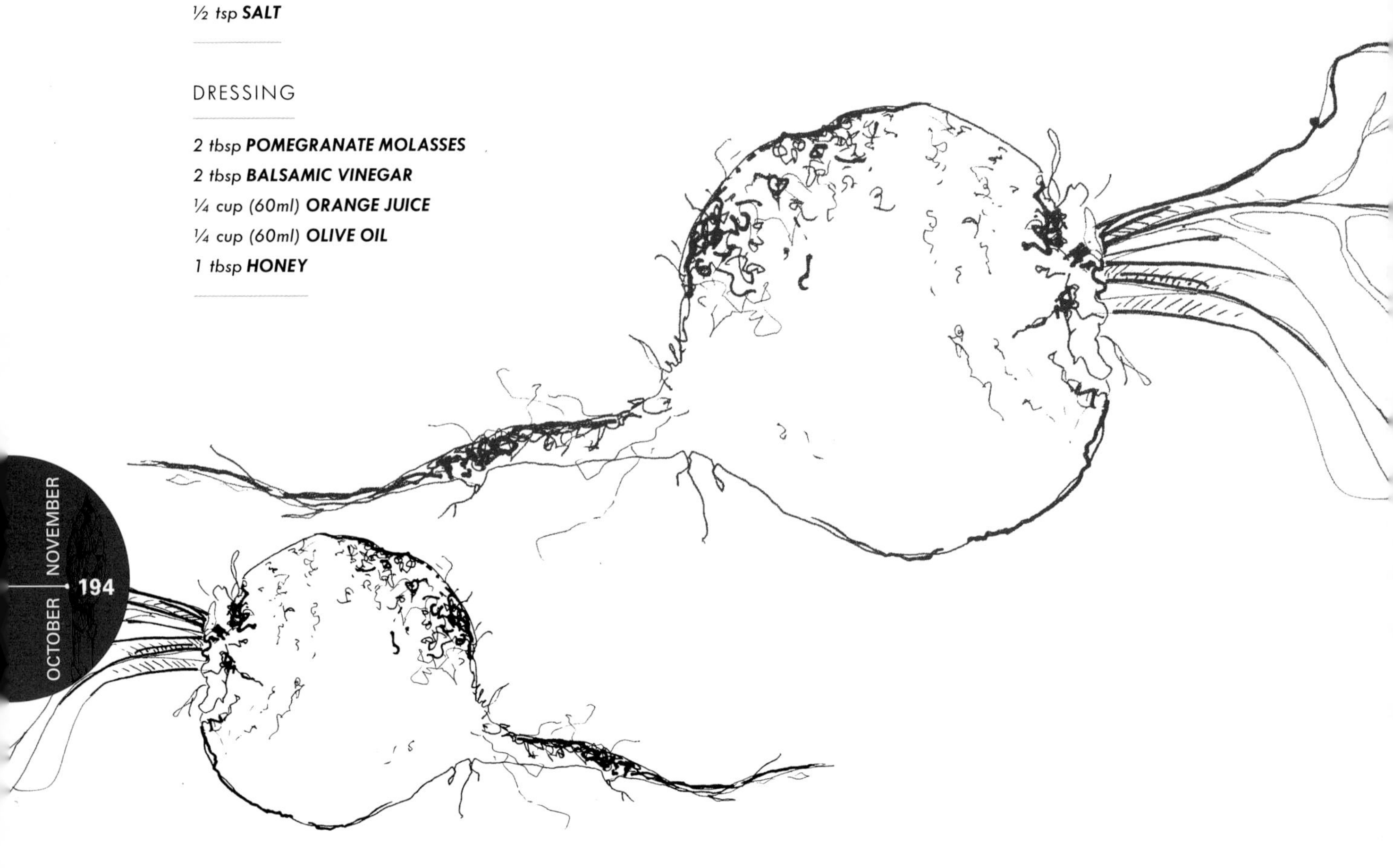

"You can beat an egg but you can't beet-a-root." – The Tupperware Queen

MAPLE WALNUT BROWNIE

*450g **DARK CHOCOLATE***
*450g **UNSALTED BUTTER***
*9 **EGGS***
*2 cups (440g) **CASTER SUGAR***
*2 tsp **VANILLA EXTRACT***
*2 cups (300g) plain **FLOUR***
*1½ cups (150g) **COCOA**, sifted*
*250g **CREAM CHEESE**, softened*
*¼ cup (90g) **MAPLE SYRUP***
*½ cup (50g) **WALNUTS**, roughly chopped*

Preheat oven to 160°C.

Grease a 20 x 30cm slice tin and line with baking paper.

In a large bowl place the chocolate and butter and melt together (see pg 207).

Be careful not to overheat and burn the chocolate. Don't stir it too often either, just let the chocolate and butter melt at their own pace.

In another large bowl, whisk together the eggs, sugar and vanilla until combined.

Sift the flour and cocoa together over the egg mixture. Mix with a metal spoon until smooth and glossy. Add the melted chocolate and butter and stir until just combined. Pour the mixture into the prepared tin.

In a bowl beat together the cream cheese and maple syrup until soft and then fold in the walnuts. Drop spoonfuls randomly over the brownie mix. Run a skewer through the cream cheese so it feathers into the brownie.

Bake for 35-40minutes or until just setting in the middle and forming a crust. Check if the brownie is ready by inserting a skewer into the centre. When removed, it should have a sticky residue clinging to it (see pg 207).

Don't over bake. It will set more once it has cooled.

BIRDSEED SLICE

*150g **RAISINS***
*120g **UNSALTED BUTTER***
*½ cup (175g) **GOLDEN SYRUP***
*½ cup (80g) soft **BROWN SUGAR***
*90g smooth **PEANUT BUTTER***
*150g **ROLLED OATS***
*150g **PUMPKIN SEEDS***
*150g **SUNFLOWER SEEDS***
*150g **SESAME SEEDS***

Preheat oven to 170°C.

Grease and line a 20 x 30cm slice tin with baking paper.

In a small bowl cover the raisins with water and leave for 20 minutes to soak and plump up. This helps to prevent them from burning.

Place a saucepan over a medium heat. Melt together the butter, golden syrup, brown sugar and peanut butter, stirring constantly until thick. Remove from the heat.

Drain the raisins. In a large bowl combine the raisins with the oats and seeds. Pour the melted butter mixture over and stir well to combine.

Press the mixture into the prepared tin. Cover with baking paper or tin foil.

Bake for 15 minutes. Remove the paper or tin foil and bake for a further 15 minutes or until golden brown.

Cut while still warm and in the tin. Place in fridge and allow to set.

"It's nutritious if not delicious." – Vincent Yogi

BANANA COCONUT CAKE

Serves 8-10

1½ cups (150g) ***DESICCATED COCONUT***
1¼ cups (300ml) ***MILK****, for soaking*
185g ***UNSALTED BUTTER****, softened*
1½ cups (330g) ***CASTER SUGAR***
3 ***EGGS***
3 ripe ***BANANAS****, mashed*
⅔ cup (160ml) ***MILK***
3 cups (450g) ***SELF RAISING FLOUR***
PASSION FRUIT PULP *(optional for serving)*
1 cup (70g) ***LONG THREAD COCONUT*** *for the topping, toasted*

CREAM CHEESE ICING

100g ***UNSALTED BUTTER****, softened*
600g ***ICING SUGAR****, sifted*
250g ***CREAM CHEESE****, softened*
JUICE *and* ***ZEST*** *of 1* ***LEMON***

Preheat oven to 180°C.

Grease and line a 26cm spring form round tin.

Place the coconut and the first measure of milk together in a bowl. Leave to soak.

In a mixing bowl cream the butter and sugar together. Add the eggs one at a time, scraping down the sides of the mixing bowl and beating well between each addition.

Once the eggs are combined, add the soaked milky coconut and mashed bananas. Mix together.

Add the second measure of milk and the flour, alternating between each.

Mix well and pour into the lined tin.

Bake for approximately 1 hour or until a skewer is inserted into the centre and comes out clean.

To prepare the cream cheese icing: in a cake mixer combine the butter and icing sugar until fine bread crumbs are formed. Add cream cheese, juice and zest. Beat on high for 5 minutes until light and fluffy.

Once the cake is cooled, ice with the cream cheese icing. Sprinkle with the toasted coconut and drizzle with a spiral of passion fruit pulp for a final flourish.

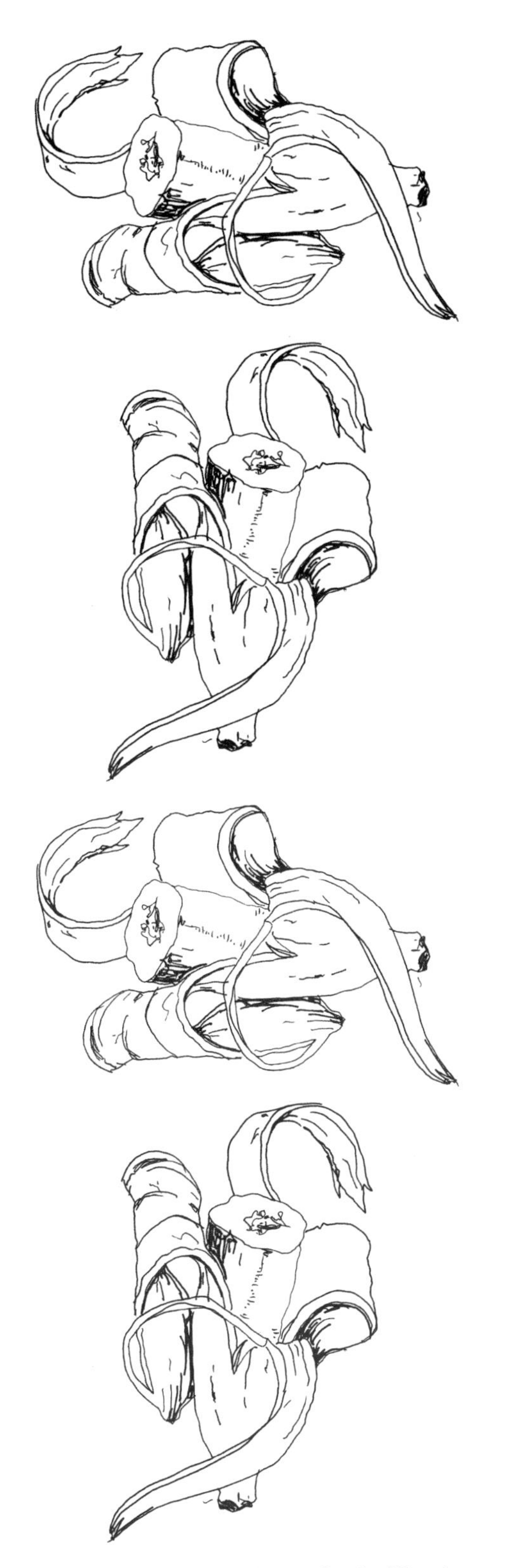

"A piece of cake!" – Anon

KUMARA CHUTNEY

We were lucky to have Jacqueline Freeman cheffing at Ripe a few years ago. This chutney and the sesame mayonnaise (see pg 205) are a couple of her recipes that we still use everyday.

Makes approximately 3 litres

*2kg **KUMARA**, any colour, roughly chopped*
*4 tbsp **CUMIN SEEDS**, toasted (see pg 211)*
*4 tbsp **CORIANDER SEEDS**, toasted*
*2 tsp **GROUND GINGER***
*5 tsp **FRESH GINGER**, grated*
*3 cloves **GARLIC**, crushed*
*3 tsp **GARAM MASALA***
*3 tsp **GROUND TURMERIC***
*3 tsp **CURRY POWDER***
*1 **ONION**, peeled, finely diced*
*800ml **CIDER VINEGAR***
*2 cups (300g) soft **BROWN SUGAR***
*2 cups (300g) **WHITE SUGAR***
*2 tsp **SALT***

To prepare the pickle: place all the ingredients except the kumara in a saucepan. Bring to the boil and simmer for 40 minutes.

In another saucepan cover the kumara with water and bring to a boil. Cook until the kumara is soft enough to mash, approximately 30 minutes. Drain and mash.

Add the cooked pickle to the mashed kumara and use a stick blender to process until smooth.

Pour the hot chutney into sterilised jars and seal (see pg 209).

RHUBARB & RAISIN CHUTNEY

Makes approximately 1 litre

*3 tbsp **OLIVE OIL***
*2 large **ONIONS**, peeled, roughly chopped*
*1 cup (250ml) **MALT VINEGAR***
*2 cups (300g) soft **BROWN SUGAR***
*1 tsp **GROUND CINNAMON***
*½ tsp **GROUND CLOVES***
*1 tsp **CHILLI POWDER***
*1 cup (160g) **RAISINS***
*3 tsp **SALT***
*750g **RHUBARB**, trimmed and cut into 1cm pieces*

Place a large saucepan over a medium heat and add the oil. Add the onions and cook for 5 minutes.

Add the rest of the ingredients and simmer over a low heat for 40 minutes.

Pour the hot chutney into sterilised jars and seal (see pg 209).

"All good things come to those who wait." – Anon

THE DRESSING ROOM

When it comes to which oils to use, we often find olive oil on its own too intense in these recipes. We recommend mixing it with a lighter vegetable oil such as rice bran, canola or sun flower oil. However, if you want to make a simple quick dressing use a good New Zealand extra virgin olive oil, with a splash of either fresh lemon juice, verjuice, vincotto or an aged balsamic vinegar.

These recipes are on the generous side. They will keep in the fridge.

MUSTARD DRESSING

JUICE** of 1 **LEMON
*½ cup (125ml) **WHITE WINE VINEGAR***
*1½ tbsp soft **BROWN SUGAR***
*1 clove **GARLIC**, crushed*
*½ cup **FRESH ITALIAN PARSLEY**, roughly chopped*
*2 tbsp **WHOLEGRAIN MUSTARD***
*2 cups (500ml) **VEGETABLE OIL***

In a small bowl, combine the lemon juice, vinegar, sugar, garlic, parsley and mustard.

Use a stick blender to blend, adding the oil last to emulsify.

BALSAMIC REDUCTION

*1½ cups **BALSAMIC VINEGAR***
*1 cup (220g) **WHITE SUGAR***

Combine the balsamic vinegar and sugar in a small saucepan over a medium heat and bring to a rapid boil for 15 minutes. Keep an eye on it, as it may overflow.

DILL DRESSING

JUICE** of 1 **LEMON
*½ cup (125ml) **WHITE WINE VINEGAR***
*1½ tbsp soft **BROWN SUGAR***
*½ cup **FRESH DILL** or chervil, roughly chopped*
*1 clove **GARLIC**, crushed*
*2 tbsp **CAPERS***
*2 tbsp **WHOLEGRAIN MUSTARD***
*2 cups (500ml) **VEGETABLE OIL***

In a small bowl combine the lemon juice, vinegar, sugar, dill, garlic, capers and mustard.

Use a stick blender to blend, adding the oil last to emulsify.

SMOKED PAPRIKA DRESSING

JUICE** of 1 **LEMON
*⅓ cup (80ml) **WHITE WINE VINEGAR***
*1 tbsp **HONEY** or 1½ tbsp soft brown sugar*
*2 tsp **DIJON MUSTARD***
*1 tbsp **SMOKED PAPRIKA***
*1½ cups (375ml) **VEGETABLE OIL***
SALT** and freshly **GROUND BLACK PEPPER

In a small bowl, combine the lemon, vinegar, honey, mustard and paprika.

Use a stick blender to blend, adding the oil last to emulsify.

Season to taste with salt and pepper.

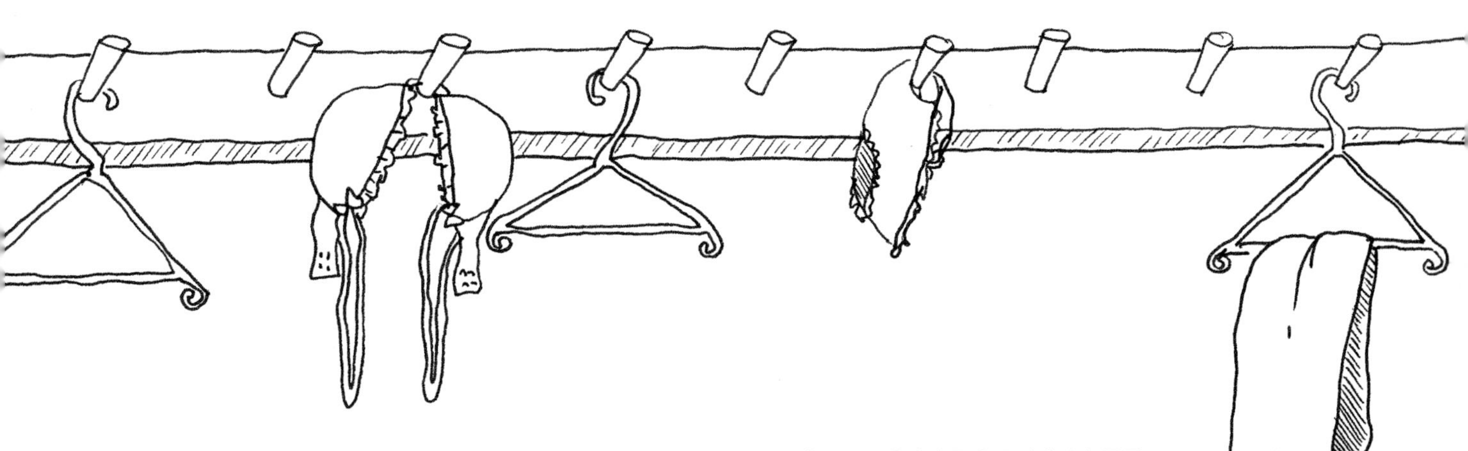

FRESH MINT DRESSING

JUICE** of 1 **LEMON
*½ cup (125ml) **WHITE WINE VINEGAR***
*1½ tbsp soft **BROWN SUGAR***
*1 clove **GARLIC**, crushed*
*½ cup **FRESH MINT LEAVES**, finely chopped*
*2 tbsp **WHOLEGRAIN MUSTARD***
*2 cups (500ml) **VEGETABLE OIL***

In a small bowl, combine the lemon juice, vinegar, sugar, garlic, mint and mustard.

Use a stick blender to blend, adding the oil last to emulsify.

FRESH MINT & ORANGE DRESSING

Follow the mint dressing recipe (above) replacing the juice of 1 lemon with the juice of 1 orange.

FRESH POMEGRANATE & MINT DRESSING

*Seeds of 1 whole **POMEGRANATE***
*3 tbsp **POMEGRANATE MOLASSES***
*1 cup (250ml) **POMEGRANATE JUICE***
*¼ cup (60ml) **VEGETABLE OIL***
*1 tbsp **LIQUID HONEY***
*½ cup **FRESH MINT LEAVES**, torn*

In a bowl place the pomegranate seeds, molasses, pomegranate juice, oil, honey and fresh mint. Mix well until the molasses dissolves, adding more honey if it needs additional sweetening.

BASIL DRESSING

*4 cups tightly packed **BASIL LEAVES**, roughly chopped*
*½ cup **WHITE WINE VINEGAR***
*2 tbsp soft **BROWN SUGAR***
*2 tbsp **DIJON MUSTARD***
*2 cloves **GARLIC**, crushed*
JUICE** of 1 **LEMON
*2 cups (500ml) **VEGETABLE OIL***
SALT** and freshly **GROUND BLACK PEPPER

In a bowl combine the basil, vinegar, brown sugar, mustard, garlic and lemon juice.

Use a stick blender to blend, while slowly pouring in the oil last to emulsify.

Season with salt and pepper.

THE DRESSING ROOM CONTINUED

TAHINI DRESSING

JUICE** of 2 **LEMONS
*¼ cup (60ml) **TAHINI***
*¼ cup (60ml) **VEGETABLE OIL***
*¼ cup (60ml) **SESAME OIL***
*2 cloves **GARLIC**, crushed*
*1 cup **FRESH CORIANDER**, finely chopped*
*2 tbsp **SESAME SEEDS**, toasted*
*1 tsp **SALT***
*1 tbsp soft **BROWN SUGAR** or honey*
*2 tbsp **WATER***

Place all ingredients into a bowl and blend with a stick blender until smooth.

YOGHURT DRESSING

*1½ cups (375ml) **PLAIN UNSWEETENED YOGHURT***
*½ cup **FRESH CORIANDER**, finely chopped*
*1 clove **GARLIC**, crushed*
*2 tbsp **SWEET CHILLI SAUCE***
*1 tbsp **CURRY POWDER***
SALT** and freshly **GROUND BLACK PEPPER

Place the yoghurt, coriander, crushed garlic, sweet chilli sauce and curry powder in a bowl. Mix and season to taste with salt and pepper.

BASIC AIOLI

Just use a light vegetable oil for this recipe

*2 **EGG YOLKS***
*1 clove **GARLIC**, crushed*
*1 tbsp **WHITE WINE VINEGAR***
*1 tsp **WHOLEGRAIN MUSTARD***
*1 tsp **LEMON JUICE***
*1½ cups (375ml) **VEGETABLE OIL***
*½ tsp **SALT***
*½ tsp freshly **GROUND BLACK PEPPER***
*1 tbsp warm **WATER***

Place the egg yolks in a blender and whiz until they change colour to a creamy, pale yellow.

Add the garlic, vinegar, mustard and lemon juice. Slowly add the oil until the eggs emulsify and the aioli becomes thick and creamy.

Season with salt and pepper.

If the aioli is too thick, add 1 tablespoon of warm water to loosen.

WASABI MAYO

*1 tbsp **WASABI PASTE***
*2 tbsp **RICE WINE VINEGAR***
*2 tsp **MIRIN***

Make the basic aioli recipe but without the whole grain mustard. Add the additional ingredients to the aioli base, mixing to combine.

SESAME MAYO

4 tbsp ***SESAME SEEDS****, toasted (see pg 211), and ground in a mortar and pestle*
1 tbsp ***RICE WINE VINEGAR***
1 tbsp light ***JAPANESE SOY SAUCE***
1 tsp ***KECAP MANIS****, sweet soy sauce*
2 tbsp ***SESAME OIL***
1 tsp ***SESAME SEEDS****, toasted*

Make the basic aioli recipe but without the wholegrain mustard. Add the additional ingredients to the aioli base, mixing to combine.

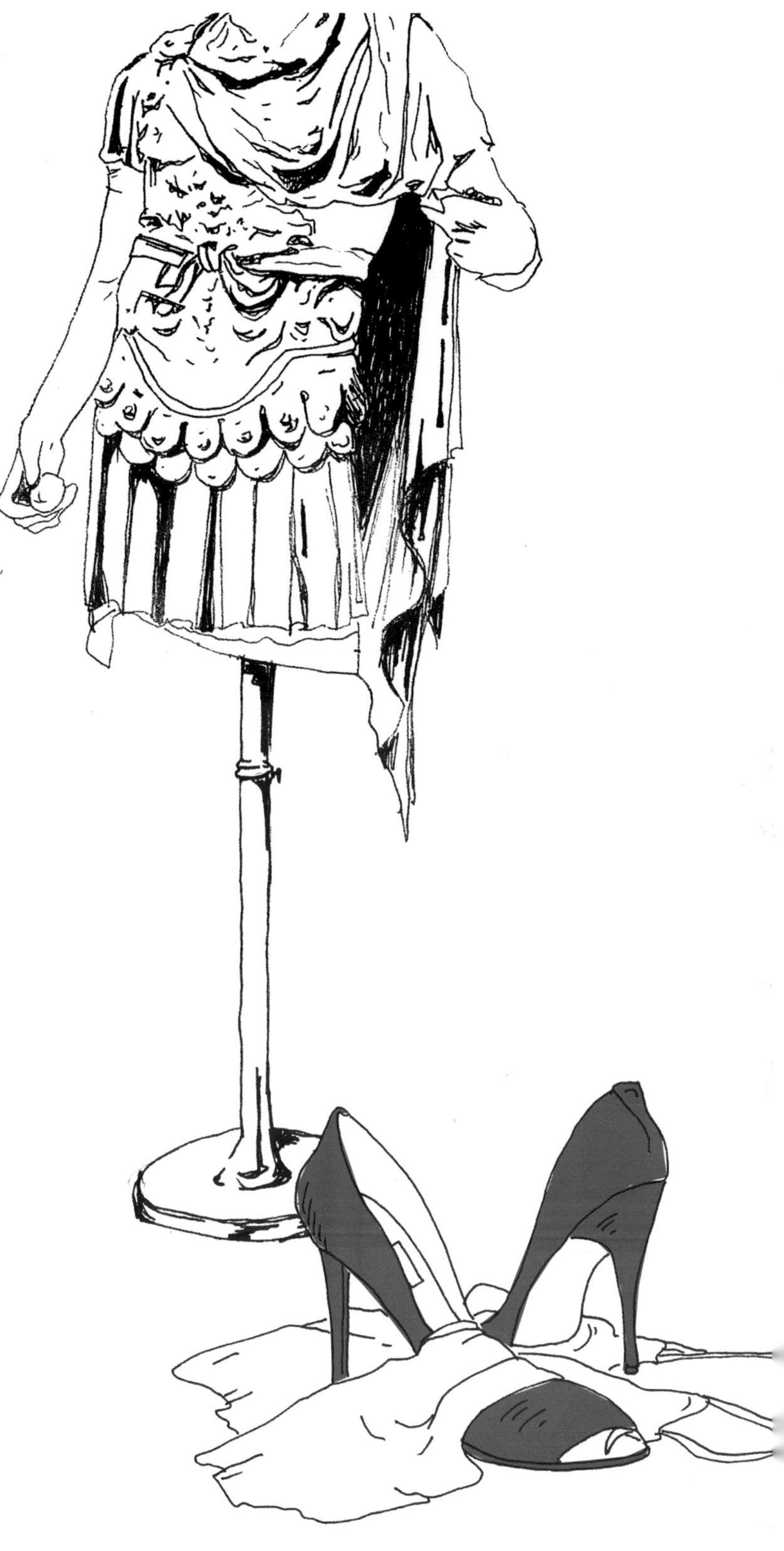

CAESAR DRESSING

Just use a light vegetable oil for this recipe

2 ***EGG YOLKS***
16 ***ANCHOVY FILLETS****, finely chopped*
2 cloves ***GARLIC****, finely chopped*
JUICE *of 2* ***LEMONS***
2 tsp ***WORCESTERSHIRE SAUCE***
2 cups (500ml) ***VEGETABLE OIL***
2-4 tbsp ***WARM WATER***
1 cup (80g) ***PARMESAN****, grated*
SALT *and freshly* ***GROUND BLACK PEPPER***

Place the egg yolks, anchovies, garlic, lemon juice and Worcestershire sauce in a bowl.

Use a stick blender to blend, while slowly pouring in the oil last to emulsify. Add water if the dressing is too thick. Stir through the Parmesan and season to taste.

You can store this dressing in the fridge for up to a week.

HOW TO'S AND TOP TIPS

BAKING

Our head baker Lynn recommends using unsalted butter in all the baking recipes. Another great tip is caster sugar, as it easily dissolves and creams with butter beautifully.

To make self raising flour add 2 teaspoons baking powder to 1 cup of plain flour.

MUFFINS

Be careful not to overmix your batter as this will result in a tough, dense muffin.

When you combine the ingredients, don't worry if you see a few wet or dry patches – portion into the tins and the oven will work it all out.

BROWNIES

The basic principle for getting a brownie to take you to a gooey giddiness is all in the cooking time. Don't turn it into a cake by overcooking it.

The brownie is ready when a thin crust has formed on the surface and a skewer comes out with lots of sticky residue on it. The brownie will have risen slightly.

The good thing about brownies is that if undercooked they're still delicious.

OVEN TEMPERATURE

Remember the temperatures will vary from oven to oven. Oven dimensions, functions and dish size all affect the end result.

When trying a recipe for the first time, keep an eye on what you are cooking. Take a peek 10 minutes before our recommended time.

CARAMELS

A sugar thermometer is very helpful when making caramel sauces and pralines, but not essential.

Look for the golden colour and caramel smell. There is something great about learning by sight and smell as well as the science behind it.

Follow the recipe closely, watching it constantly. Once the sugar reaches approximately 122°C, it all happens very quickly. Don't be tempted to stir the sugar as it may crystallise.

THE SUGAR TEMPERATURE MEASURE

To test caramel without a thermometer use the hard ball method. Hard ball occurs at approximately 122°C. Drop a ½ teaspoon of the mixture into some cold water. If it forms a hard ball the sugar is ready to make praline.

CHOCOLATE

Chocolate icing for cakes gets a lift in flavour with a squeeze of lemon juice.

Try melting chocolate either of these ways: place a heatproof bowl over a saucepan of simmering water. Add the chocolate. Once it has warmed and is turning glossy, stir it and remove saucepan from heat. The chocolate will continue to melt after you have taken it off the heat.

Alternatively, use your microwave and heat on high in short bursts, 10-15 seconds at a time.

A little tip: chocolate seizes or goes grainy when it's too hot. If this happens, stir a dash of oil into it.

Using a good quality chocolate with a high percentage of cocoa really does make a difference to the flavour.

CINNAMON CREAM

To make whipped cinnamon cream, pour 300ml of cream into a bowl with 2 teaspoons of sieved icing sugar and a ½ teaspoon of ground cinnamon. Whisk until thick.

EGG WHITES

Don't throw away egg whites. Freeze them in a plastic bag. Make sure you label the date and quantity. Defrost and return egg whites to room temperature before use. When whisking egg whites it is important to start with a dry clean bowl. Grease and water are the possible culprits if you aren't getting any volume when whisking. Don't use a plastic bowl as these can harbour hidden oils.

Run a cut lemon around the bowl before adding the egg whites. The lemon helps to increase volume and stiffness.

When making meringue, initially whisk the egg whites alone. When they have achieved a good stiffness, slowly add sugar. Allow the sugar crystals to begin to dissolve before adding more.

A good meringue base recipe is 2 egg whites to ½ cup caster sugar.

PASTRY MAKING

Some key things:

- Have the butter as cold as possible. Handle the raw mixture as little as possible and chill pastry before rolling. Also, chill pastry after you have lined your tins as this relaxes the gluten, preventing tough pastry and shrinkage.

- If you are not using a food processor, use your fingertips to combine the butter and flour.

- When using a food processor, pulse the mix until bread crumbs are formed.

- Add the minimum amount of chilled water – don't add more water too soon and allow for differences between flours and their absorption rates.

SWEET PASTRY RECIPE

Makes enough for 24 small tarts or 1 x 26cm fluted tart tins

330g plain flour
180g unsalted butter, cold cut into small cubes
100g icing sugar
¼ tsp salt
1 egg yolk
2 tbsp cold water

Place the flour, butter, icing sugar and salt into the bowl of a food processor. Pulse together until you achieve a coarse bread crumb consistency. Add the egg yolk and water and pulse just until the dough comes together. You may need to add a little bit of extra water.

Remove from the bowl and shape into a smooth disc. Wrap in cling film and chill in the fridge until ready to use.

BLIND BAKING

Preheat oven to 180°C

Blind baking will ensure the pastry is cooked correctly and evenly. Choose either of these methods for preparing a blind baked pastry shell.

NOTE: If making mini tart shells reduce the cooking time as per the recipe.

Prick pastry bottom all over with a fork – this will stop any bubbling – then lay a sheet of baking paper onto the pastry. Weigh it down with ceramic baking beads, rice or dried pulses and bake for 15 minutes. Remove the weights and paper and bake for another 10-15 minutes.

Alternatively, use a sheet of tin foil pressed down lightly onto the pastry base and bake for 15 minutes. Remove foil and bake for another 10-15 minutes.

JAMS, CHUTNEY, STERILISING AND SEALING

STERILISING JARS FOR PRESERVING, JAMMING & PICKLING

These are some of the best methods to get your jars ready to successfully store your preserves. If you can't find a matching lid to your jar use the clear plastic preserving seals that you can get from the supermarket. Bottle your jams, curds, preserves and chutneys while jars are warm.

Microwave method: ¼ fill your jars with hot water and microwave them on high for 10 minutes.

Oven method: The more traditional and conventional method for sterilising jars involves a good wash in warm soapy water. Rinse and then let dry upside down in a cool oven (120°C) for 30 minutes or until you need to use them.

SETTING TIMES FOR JAMS AND CURD

Jam setting point methods:

- Drop a little jam on a saucer and push it with your finger. If it wrinkles, the jam has reached setting point.
- If you own a sugar thermometer, 105°C is the setting temperature for jams and jellies.

When making a citrus curd, be patient. If the curd gets too hot, you can cook the egg or split the curd.
A constant medium heat whilst stirring works well.

When the curd is starting to thicken it is ready to test. Dip a wooden spoon into the curd. Run a line with your finger through the curd on the back of the spoon. If the line holds the curd will set.

When making fruit jam the pectin and acid content affects the variance in setting time. The higher the pectin the better the set. Low acid fruit will benefit from 2 tablespoons of lemon juice to 1kg raw fruit. Soaking fruit with a little lemon juice can also help.

SEALING PRESERVES

Either seal your jars when the preserve is hot or cover them with a clean dry cloth and allow to cool first. Ensure with both methods that the jar is filled right to the top, leaving no room for moisture to form.

MEASUREMENTS AND UTENSILS

- Use an accurate set of measuring cups. Cup measures are level and not tightly packed.
- All spoon measures are level.
- Use scales that measure in grams and are large enough to weigh up to 5kgs.
- Always weigh butter. Don't rely on pack markings.

EQUIPMENT SIZES

- Slice tins – 20 x 30cm
- Sponge roll tin – 25 x 38cm
- Cake tins either 24cm or 26cm spring form
- 26cm fluted tart tin
- Deep sided pie dish 25cm
- "Lasagne" style rectangular deep sided dish

These are the sizes used in the recipes. Variance in size affects the height and depth of the end result. Experiment with what you have.

TOOLS THAT MAKE YOUR LIFE EASIER

- Sharp knives, zester and Microplane
- Sharp vegetable peeler
- Metal sieve
- Small sieve for icing sugar and cocoa
- A strong good quality whisk
- Measuring jugs, spoons and cups
- Scales that can tare to zero
- Set of ring cutters for pastry
- Small cast iron pans
- Ovenproof frying pan – 24-26cm diameter, excellent for making tarte tatin
- Wooden spoon and spatulas
- Metal spoons
- Good can opener
- Food processor and stick blender
- Electric mixer
- Mortar and pestle

DEGLAZING

Deglazing is the process of adding stock or alcohol to a very hot pan. This will loosen the cooking juices that have solidified on the bottom.

DRIED PULSES

- Dried beans: adzuki, black eyed, borlotti, butter (lima), cannellini, haricot, mung, pinto and red kidney.
- Dried peas: chickpea, green or yellow split peas.
- Dried lentils: red, brown or green (puy).

COOKING GUIDELINES FOR DRIED PULSES

Overnight soaking is recommended for all pulses, particularly for chickpeas and red kidney beans.

Exceptions to the soaking rule are split red lentils and puy which are very small and cook successfully without prior soaking.

Always wash pulses carefully before cooking as they may contain small stones and other unwanted matter.

Be sure to drain off the soaking water and cook in fresh water. This reduces the build up of digestive gases.

Add salt near the end of cooking time to avoid tough skins.

APPROXIMATE COOKING TIMES	
20-30 minutes	Puy lentil, red lentil
30-60 minutes +	Adzuki, black eyed bean, brown lentil, split pea
60-90 minutes +	Haricot, cannellini, butter bean, chickpea, red kidney

Soaking does reduce the cooking time somewhat for all the beans, so be sure to check in order to cook to your liking.

FOR ALL PULSES

- 1 cup dried = 2½-3 cups cooked
- 1 cup to 6-8 cups water

Soak pulses overnight if necessary. Drain, rinse and bring to the boil. Skim any frothy residue off the top.

GRAINS, PASTA AND RICE – COOKING AND GUIDELINES

BUCKWHEAT GROATS

- ½ cup un-toasted buckwheat groats = 1 cup cooked
- 1 cup untoasted buckwheat groats to 2 cups water

In a large saucepan add 1 tablespoon vegetable oil to toast 1 cup of groats. Cook for a minute.

Add boiling water and cover the pot. Reduce to a simmer and cook for 15 minutes or until the water is absorbed,

Remove from heat and leave to stand for 5 minutes before removing the lid.

BULGHUR WHEAT

- 1 cup bulghur = 2 cups soaked
- 1 cup bulghur to 2 cups water

Rinse the bulghur. Place in a large bowl and pour over boiling water. Cover and leave to sit for 20-40 minutes. Bulghur wheat is available in various grain sizes, so soaking time will vary. It needs to be soft but not mushy. Squeeze out extra moisture with a clean tea towel and fluff up with a fork.

COUSCOUS

A bay leaf, or vegetable or chicken stock is a great way to flavour the couscous.

- 1 cup dried = 3 cups soaked
- 1 cup couscous to 1 cup boiling water or liquid stock

In a large heatproof bowl place the couscous, a pinch of salt, freshly ground pepper and a dash of oil.

Stir though and smoothe down to achieve a level surface. Pour boiling water or stock over the couscous and cover with cling film and set aside for 10 minutes. Remove cling film and separate any clumps with a fork.

ISRAELI COUSCOUS

- 1 cup dried = 2½ cups cooked
- 1 cup to 4 cups water

Cook in boiling salted water for approximately 10 minutes. Drain and refresh under cold water. Drain again and squeeze out excess moisture with a clean tea towel.

ORZO

- 1 cup dried = 3 cups cooked
- 1 cup to 5 cups water

Cook in boiling salted water for approximately 10 minutes. Drain and refresh under cold water. Drain again and squeeze out excess moisture with a clean tea towel. Mix through 1 teaspoon of olive oil to stop orzo sticking together.

PEARL BARLEY

- 1 cup dried pearl barley = 2½ cups cooked
- 1 cup pearl barley to 5 cups water or stock

Cook in boiling salted water for approximately 15 minutes. Drain and refresh under cold water. Drain again and squeeze out excess moisture with a clean tea towel.

QUINOA

- 1 cup dried = 3 cups cooked
- 1 cup quinoa to 4 cups water

Quinoa has a higher amount of protein than other grains and can be used in the same way as rice.

Wash the grains until the water runs clear. Simmer for approximately 10 minutes or until the grains are translucent.

Drain using a fine sieve and refresh under cold water. Drain and press gently with a clean tea towel to remove excess moisture. Set aside until ready to use.

RICE – LONG GRAIN (BASMATI / JASMINE)

Absorption method:

- 1 cup rice = 3 cups cooked
- 1 cup rice to 2 cups water

Rice and water must be measured accurately for the absorption method to be successful.

Wash in cold water and drain rice to remove excess starch. Continue doing this until the water is running clear. Heat a dash of vegetable oil in a saucepan over a high heat. Add the rice and stir for about 30 seconds. Pour boiling water (cup measured amount) over the rice and simmer gently for 12 minutes, covered.

Remove from heat still covered, and allow to stand for 10-12 minutes before removing the lid.

RICE – BROWN, WILD AND RED

These types of rice take longer to cook than white rice. Wash wild rice and soak for at least 2 hours before cooking.

- 1 cup rice = 3 cups cooked
- 1 cup rice to 6-8 cups water

Wash rice to remove excess starch, rinse and drain.

Pour the rice into the water and bring to the boil. Lower the heat and boil gently uncovered for 25-30 minutes.

You may need to add extra hot water to these types of rice as the cooking takes 2-3 times longer.

Drain the rice and rinse in cold water if using in salads.

STOCK RECIPE USING POWDERED STOCK

We recommend using liquid stock or the Vegeta Gourmet powdered stock range.

- 1 teaspoon powder to 1 cup hot water

Of course making your own stock is great, but we haven't included recipes for these as all our recipes are tested with liquid and powdered stock.

TOASTING NUTS AND SEEDS

Toasting intensifies flavour. Try either of these ways: in a small dry frying pan over a high heat, toast the nuts or seeds. Keep them moving until some of the following things happen: a fragrant smell, popping sounds or a golden colour. This happens very quickly. You can also toast nuts and seeds in the oven set at a medium heat (160°C) for around 5 minutes. Keep an eye on them.

CONVERSION CHARTS

Different measurements and conversions are used around the world. For example, the general agreement is that 28.35 grams is equal to 1 ounce. However, in New Zealand 25 grams is often used as the equivalent to 1 ounce.

On this page we have provided a range of conversions as well as some that are specific to *Ripe Recipes*. Whatever measurement system you use, keep it consistent and there will be a greater chance the recipe will be a success.

CONVERSIONS SPECIFIC TO RIPE RECIPES	
1 cup soft brown sugar	160g (6 oz)
1 cup white or caster sugar	220g (8 oz)
1 cup plain, self-rising or wholewheat flour	150g (5 oz)
1 cup icing sugar	150g (5 oz)
1 cup cocoa powder	100g (4oz)
1 cup basil, parsley, coriander, baby spinach, rocket & mint	40g (1.4oz)
1 cup Parmesan cheese grated	80g (3oz)

OVEN TEMPERATURE			
	Celsius	Fahrenheit	Gas mark
low	130	275	1
cool	150	300	2
	160	325	3
moderate	180	350	4
	190	375	5
fairly hot	200	400	6
	220	425	7
	230	450	8
hot	250	475	9
very hot	260	500	10

Grams		Ounces
Precise	Range	
28	25 - 30	1
56	50 - 60	2
84	75 - 90	3
112	100 - 120	4
140	125 - 150	5
168	150 - 180	6
196	175 - 210	7
224	200 - 240	8
252	225 - 270	9
280	250 - 300	10
308	275 - 330	11
336	300 - 360	12
364	325 - 390	13
392	350 - 420	14
420	375 - 450	15
448	400 - 480	16 (1 lb)

NOTES

INDEX

C

M

N

O

P

Q

R

S

T

V

W

Y

We would like to acknowledge and thank the authors and publishers of the photographed books (opposite) which have been an inspiration to us at Ripe over the years.

Digby Law's PICKLE & CHUTNEY COOKBOOK
ONE YEAR AT BOOKS FOR COOKS No. 2
FEAST NIGELLA LAWSON
LADIES, A PLATE Traditional home baking ALEXA JOHNSTON
ROSE CARRARINI BREAKFAST · LUNCH · TEA ROSE BAKERY
David Rosengarten THE DEAN & DELUCA COOKBOOK
NIGEL SLATER REAL COOKING
PEGGY PORSCHEN Cake chic
Peter Gordon a culinary journey
JAMIE OLIVER The Return of the Naked Chef
TED SMART
SALLY CLARKE'S BOOK
Recipes from a Restaurant, Shop & Bakery
THE NEW ZEALAND COOK'S BIBLE
OTTOLENGHI
INGREDIENTS & RECIPES LEON ALLEGRA McEVEDY
She's Leaving Home Monica Trapaga
HESTON BLUMENTHAL
The Fat Duck Cookbook

THANK YOU

As the saying goes – you're only as good as the people around you and this couldn't be more true of Ripe. My great co-workers have not only allowed me to grow the business but have also allowed me to step away from the daily operations of Ripe so that I could concentrate on this book.

Most of this book is the work of two very talented ladies. Their dedication to the cause has gone above and beyond the call of duty, and their patience and understanding throughout the process has made my job a lot easier.

Firstly, Karla Granville – Karla and lists go together like wine and cheese and thank goodness for that, because without her organisational skills, enthusiasm and creativity this book would not have happened. A big thank you also goes out to her family for putting up with her absenteeism while she dedicated her time to this project. Ripe is a better place with you in it Karla. I am very lucky to have such a good shoulder to lean on!

Secondly, Michelle Ineson, my shop manager and illustrative genius. Working with you at Ripe has been a true pleasure. Your illustrations and talents are far above even your own expectations. Thank you for adding your creative flair and bringing this book to life.

Lynn Colbert – Lynn, you've been with me since the very beginning, not only baking your heart out everyday for Ripe but also producing some delicious recipes for this book. Thank you for your continuing support.

Andrea Saunders – for creating the array of amazing salad recipes, not just for this book but for Ripe in general. And if you think that's good, wait until you hear her sing! Such a talented lady.

Pip Wylie, Kylie Wilson and Louise Kelleher – for all your input, advice and recipe contributions, and ensuring the kitchen ran smoothly during this chaotic time.

John-Henry Rand, John Utumapu, Tina Brown, Gemma Heffernan and Bik Yimdee for all your recipe contributions and for cooking up a storm everyday in the ripe kitchen.

Amy Melchior – thank you for stepping in and taking over the reins in perfecting and testing all the recipes. Your calm and composed manner gave me complete reassurance. Thank you for all your delicious recipes too. You were the icing on the cake.

To all Ripe employees for keeping the shop running while we caused havoc around you. Your support and contributions in all shapes and sizes have been much appreciated.

Our trustworthy suppliers, especially Art of Produce for your assistance with the seasonality goal, Skellonz for pomegranate seeds, and Altezano for all the wonderful coffee that keeps us going!

Fran Holland – you took the words right out of my mouth. Literally.

Sally Cameron – thank you for your exceptional advice, critiquing and feedback.

Megan Dunbar – I couldn't have asked for a more beautiful test kitchen and appreciate all your feedback.

Jo Bridgeford – for your bake off!

Nicole Beaver, along with many others, for helping with the arduous task of editing Ripe Recipes.

Jude Mewburn – for helping me when I needed it.

Sally Greer, Colette Sherley and Tamara Darragh at Beatnik – for seeing our vision and turning it into Ripe Recipes with your design, photography and publishing nous.

To those – you know who you are – featuring in photographs throughout Ripe Recipes!

There are also a few people I would like to thank who have influenced and supported me over the years:

Jane Mary McCulloch – you are a true friend and perfect work colleague. Thank you for all your help and support during those early years at "baby" Ripe.

Josh Dalton – for telling me I could do it on my own (just when I needed to hear it), and for all your building skills "at the drop of a hammer".

My father Andrew Redfern – thanks for all the business advice and loaning me money when the chips were down.

My mother Jane Redfern for passing on her love for food, support and fridges!

Simone Crowe – for your amazing eye and for designing such a beautiful store.

Gawain Cowley – thank you for your many years of hard work cooking madly in both stores. Your transition from "baby" Ripe to "bigger" Ripe was impressive. Mint and pea purée forever!

Claire Baker– for being an office angel and Matthew Griffin for spreadsheets.

Ginny Kevey – "a beautiful lady".

To all the many talented people that have worked at Ripe since it opened in 2002 and contributed to its success and to this book in any way.

To my friends and family who encouraged, supported and helped me through all the ups and downs of starting and running a business and, well, life in general.

And most humble thanks to all the Ripe customers, who bring us so much pleasure and brighten all our days.

ripe

"Don't let it end like this, tell them I said something."
– Pancho Villa 1877-1923 (last words)

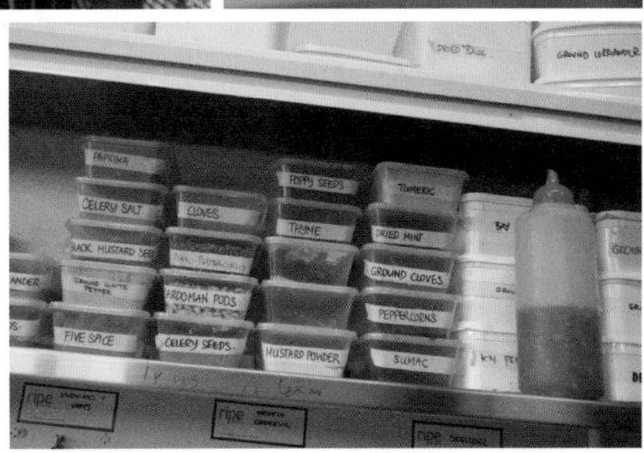

PAPRIKA
POPPY SEEDS
TUMERIC
CELERY SALT
CLOVES
THYME
DRIED MINT
GROUND CLOVES
PEPPERCORNS
FIVE SPICE
CELERY SEEDS
MUSTARD POWDER
SUMAC

olives